T0308426

THE
TOBACCONIST
HANDBOOK

THE
TOBACCONIST
HANDBOOK

AN ESSENTIAL GUIDE TO
CIGARS & PIPES

JORGE ARMENTEROS, CMT

Skyhorse Publishing

Skyhorse Publishing books may be purchased in bulk at special discounts for sales promotion, corporate gifts, fund-raising, or educational purposes. Special editions can also be created to specifications. For details, contact the Special Sales Department, Skyhorse Publishing, 307 West 36th Street, 11th Floor, New York, NY 10018 or info@skyhorsepublishing.com.

Skyhorse® and Skyhorse Publishing® are registered trademarks of Skyhorse Publishing, Inc.®, a Delaware corporation.

Visit our website at www.skyhorsepublishing.com.

10 9 8 7 6 5 4 3

Library of Congress Cataloging-in-Publication Data is available on file.

Jacket design by 5mediadesign
Front jacket photographs: Getty Images
Back jacket photograph courtesy of the author

Print ISBN: 978-1-5107-5212-2
Ebook ISBN: 978-1-5107-5213-9

Printed in China

The heart and soul of the luxury tobacco industry lies with those who have a true passion for the product and the value it adds to real lives. Real passion is quiet and humble; not something that can be measured by cigar selfies, social media likes, or the size of your cigar collection. This book is inspired by, and dedicated to the people whose passion for luxury cigars and pipes is the least interesting thing about them.

TABLE OF CONTENTS

FOREWORD
by J. Glynn Loope

Given that I am a creature of the legislative and political process, I all too often conduct my conversations and writing in such language. Even though I spend every day fighting the bureaucratic state, I still have a habit of sounding like a bureaucrat. So this introduction won't be any different.

I scan the occupational postings, and find it so intriguing that many professions expect and require practitioners to obtain a license or permit to even have a given job. Now, as one with a libertarian bent on government interference in our lives, I have to pause and think, "It's a good thing for my electrician, plumber, or other contractor to be licensed; it lets me know that they studied for their chosen profession." Then I look at the list again, and I think about my wife going to the nail salon to visit the cosmetologist, or remember my father taking me to the local barber. Both studied to get the skills for their profession.

Flash forward. What began as a fondness for premium cigars grew into a passion. I was blessed to have a local cigar shop that is now over a hundred years old, Milan Tobacconists in the Blue Ridge Mountains of Virginia. An establishment with a national and indeed global reputation for blending great pipe tobacco, they recommended my first cigar, and have been recommending to me for nearly two decades. In thinking about this foreword for *The Tobacconist Handbook*, I again paused to think about what makes a great tobacconist great.

I have traveled to premium cigar shops in every region of the nation, and thankfully, there seems to be a "common ground" where the tobacconist and consumer meet. They meet on the expectation that not only will the products be enjoyed, and worth the investment, but that the service will be memorable. In those establishments that provide a lounge or similar atmosphere like a full cigar bar or any full-service business that promotes "the cigar culture," there is, again, common ground where all of these establishments meet: service, atmosphere, professionalism, quality products, and expert advice.

Those who are passionate for great cigars and premium tobacco have long memories, and they like to talk about their experiences. That should be remembered by anyone who wants to be in this business. Also, during the course of my national travels, I hear every day about consumer experiences.

I often receive calls and texts from friends or random consumers through Cigar Rights of America with questions like "Where should I go to enjoy a cigar in [Nashville, Minneapolis, Atlanta, Omaha, etc.]?" and I have that list based upon truly memorable experiences, all in local cigar shops. That means someone is making money off one cigar consumer's great moment. That's how word spreads, and that's how small businesses thrive.

I was once walking with my friend Ron Melendi, a Tobacconist University Certified Master Tobacconist (CMT), and there was a Starbucks attached to the cigar shop in front of us. We began discussing how they got the public to buy an expensive cup of coffee. First, I love their mantra, "We are the place between work and home, or 'The Third Place.'" It should be adopted by every cigar shop in the land. The next critical ingredient is expert knowledge of their product and, finally, a memorable experience. Even though many have had challenges in that regard, always having that as your objective will make you better in this—or any—business.

Which leads me full circle to where this discussion began—training experts who have a passion for premium tobacco. Tobacconist University is the only training program of its kind that seeks to establish standards for the premium tobacconist, and the unique initiative to certify the knowledge of the passionate consumer.

This book, and the associated training programs available through Tobacconist University, will take you on a journey. You will experience and feel the culture of these products, from the fields and factories of Latin America, through the practice of serving a discerning public with the finest cigars or pipe tobacco in the world. The aspiring tobacconist will learn of the use for the important accoutrements used by the profession, and how you convey this knowledge, and appreciation, to the novice consumer.

That's the way I would like the reader of this handbook to approach this narrative—as a journey. It is impossible for any given book to capture the essence of premium tobacco, but *The Tobacconist Handbook* will introduce the history of those golden leaves, and the basics of their nurturing, from seed to shelf.

But this is also a personal journey for the aspiring tobacconist, or those who crave continuing education. One of the nuances of this industry that captures me the most is imagination. Learning or imagining how manufacturers of these great products maintain consistency, or develop a new blend, or how the *certified tobacconist* may develop their own blends one day, by either working with a great producer of cigars, or tinkering with a kitchen full of pipe tobacco. It's also about learning what the consumer appreciates or desires, and how the professional tobacconist can meet and exceed their expectations.

I believe this book can guide that journey into the world of premium tobacco, and I also believe Tobacconist University sets the standard for the education of this profession. It is what sets premium tobacco apart from other products. It's like what I say every year at the *Cigar Aficionado* Big Smoke seminars in Las Vegas: "Only in the world of premium cigars would five hundred people get up for 9:00 a.m. classes in, of all places, Las Vegas, just to learn more about this passion we share!"

Well, you are doing the same by reading this book. You're proving that this is a different and special passion, and that you want to be a part of a unique pursuit that demands new skills, deep knowledge, and a commitment to continuous learning, just as that golden leaf is always evolving as well.

Enjoy this journey.

THE TWENTY-FIRST CENTURY TOBACCONIST AND PUBLIC POLICY

"The Necessary Evil" by J. Glynn Loope, Executive Director, Cigar Rights of America

In 2006, a small coalition of community tobacconists began meeting in Virginia in response to the introduction of the first proposed statewide smoking ban in the legislature. Indeed, it is somewhat ironic that in the land that is the birthplace of the nation in many respects thanks to the "currency" of tobacco, that the political winds would activate such a discussion and movement, but it did, like in so many other regions of the nation.

I was assisting with the effort primarily because I had a passionate feeling: "How dare the General Assembly tell us we can't enjoy a cigar at our favorite local bar—which welcomed us?" At one of our group meetings I told these retailers, "You are no longer just tobacconists, you are advocates. You now have to put public policy in your job description." And that is my advice to tobacconists throughout the nation.

The "simple" statement is this: if you want to protect your livelihood as a professional tobacconist, you have to be engaged in the political process. Not to belabor the history of the anti-smoking movement, but specifically in the arena of premium tobacco products, the industry is playing a game of thirty-year catch-up. But catching up is possible.

The threats in this era are more severe than at any time in history, primarily due to the launch of and battle against draconian federal regulation of the industry. Once Congress passed and the president signed the Family Smoking Prevention and Tobacco Control Act, the gates were open to unprecedented levels of regulation. The US Food and Drug Administration was granted sweeping authority to regulate all tobacco, and in 2016 it began its charge after cigars and pipe tobacco. There is also a little-known codicil that allows states and localities to go further than the federal statute.

While not addressing the over four hundred pages of regulations, I encourage the community tobacconist to review the history and current state of the regulations. However, this narrative is also about the effort to combat these onerous rules. The representative trade associations for the industry are addressing this modern-day attempt at prohibition in the halls of Congress, in the presidents' administrations (past, current, and future), and in the courts.

The threat to the livelihood of the community retail tobacconist does not flow just from Washington, DC, but from the local city hall and state capitol. Just as if the 2006 smoking ban in Virginia was their "wake-up call," numerous other states had already experienced such an epiphany. Here is a list of some of the more notable policy measures that threaten the local tobacco shop:

- **Smoking bans:** They can always get worse. Local and state governments enjoy amending and revisiting smoking policies because it gives the appearance that they are doing something. The ultimate threat is banning smoking IN premium tobacco shops. A "no exemption" policy is in the playbook of our opposition, and numerous nonprofits and many in the political community are pursuing such measures. They are also attacking patio and outdoor smoking in sweeping ways, in addition to mandating free-standing buildings in order to have smoking "privileges." Any smoking ban proposal has to be closely monitored.

- **Tax increases:** As government at all levels continuously searches for new revenue sources, tobacco is always on the short list of targets. Local and state Other Tobacco Products (OTP) taxes have to be addressed, and specifically state legislation that grants local governments more latitude to set their own rates. The new wave of legislation is more concerning on both the tax and smoking ban fronts—allowing the public to decide. Numerous states, recently, have attempted to have tobacco tax increases and smoking bans decided by public referendum. Such measures are very difficult to defeat, and expensive to take on.

- **New store locations and expansions:** A new approach to "tobacco control" is the use of zoning and building codes to regulate where a shop can be located, and if smoking will even be allowed there. Existing and prospective shops need to be diligent in monitoring local planning regulations, whereas there are national examples of shops losing their smoking privileges and halting expansion plans or attempts to create new shops, because of local planning regulations.

- **Flavored tobacco bans:** Primarily due to products not in the premium sector, numerous shops, especially those with a strong pipe and premium pipe tobacco business, have been directly threatened by local and state flavored tobacco bans. It is imperative that policy makers become familiar with the differences in products, and specifically with issues such as demographic appeal.

- **Nicotine:** The regulation of nicotine has become the umbrella under which to attack all forms of tobacco. The latest set of proposals is to regulate employee hiring practices based upon required testing, in both the public and private sectors. Such policies can affect the existing and prospective patrons of shops, and these measures are beginning to be introduced coast to coast.

- **Prohibition:** No joke. The city of Beverly Hills, California, has become the first local government in the nation to ban the sale of tobacco. A concerted effort was needed to obtain exemptions for a couple of premium cigar shops and a private cigar club, but that is not a battle that the industry needs spreading state to state, and indeed city hall to city hall.

What can I do?

Engagement with your elected officials, at multiple levels, is critical to the survival of the modern day premium tobacconist. You have to know them personally, and they need to know you. The patrons of the local shop need to be recognized as an actual constituency. The following are steps that need to be taken to protect the modern-day premium tobacconist from the ever-threatening role of government:

- Go meet your elected officials. All of them. Now. From city hall to the state capitol, introduce yourself; tell them what you do, and how you expect them to protect your interests. Also, go to the district offices for both of your US Senators and your member of the US House of Representatives. Review the issues, have a handout ready, schedule a meeting, and remember, this is not about tobacco or smoke

. . . it's about small business, property rights, and personal choice.

- When issues arise, be engaged. If it's a local issue, be at the public hearings and invite your customers. If you're a patron, round up your local enthusiasts and attend the hearings and sessions for a vote. Smoking bans and tax increases have been defeated due to "having more people in the room."

- Always email and call your elected officials, even if you don't need them "today." When issues arise, you already need to be a known commodity in the community, either as a shop owner or patron. Launch petition campaigns and call-in campaigns and host a Cigar Town Hall, where you invite elected officials into your local shop, club or lounge.

- Know the issues. The studies are now on the side of premium cigars. Youth access is not the issue with premium cigars; inhalation, addiction, and mortality studies determine that the figures are statistically insignificant. It's a hobby, not a habit. The message is, "we are different."

- Join! Be an active member of Cigar Rights of America, the Premium Cigar Association, and the state association of community tobacconists. This presents access to information, resources, technical assistance, advocacy support and the national development of a network of like-minded brethren that believe in, and will fight for, the enjoyment of perfectly legal tobacco products.

It has been said that we are living in a renaissance era of cigar making, specifically. The larger producers are generating some of the most enjoyable blends in industry history, and small-batch, or boutique, producers are pushing the envelope with innovation and creativity. In order for this artisan culture to be preserved, engagement in legislative affairs is the "new normal" for the community tobacconist and patron alike.

Go to: CigarRights.org and premiumcigars.org for additional information.

FOREWORD FROM 2009 EDITION
by Jorge Padrón

I had the good fortune of being born into a family with a long, rich tobacco tradition. Five generations of Padróns have been part of the tobacco industry for almost 150 years. The cigar industry has been part of my life since I was a child, playing in my father's Little Havana factory. I have witnessed many changes, from the types of products offered in the marketplace to sales and marketing strategies. The one constant has been the crucial role that retail tobacconists play in educating consumers and ensuring that they have access to quality products. I have often been asked to explain what makes a successful tobacconist. The answer for me lies in the same philosophy we practice daily at Padrón Cigars—the focus should be on quality, not quantity. By this I mean that it is not necessarily the biggest store or walk-in humidor that makes a tobacconist great, it is the quality of the employees that makes the difference. Tobacconists that understand their customers' needs and preferences, and who pair that with the perfect product for that particular smoker, are successful at what they do. These are the tobacconists that establish credibility and earn the trust of their consumers. Quality tobacconists will build a loyal base of customers that know they can depend on them—this is the cornerstone of any successful business.

Padrón Cigars has been careful in guiding the growth of our company in order to maintain consistent quality. For my family, it has never been about reaching larger sales numbers and greater output, but rather obtaining higher standards of quality. For us, achieving quality means delivering it consistently. This is the criteria we use in selecting tobacconists to represent our products. We look for tobacconists that share the same passion for our products; this is more important to us than the size of the store or the volume of business. Over the years we have built strong relationships with some excellent tobacconists. They have been crucial in the development of the Padrón brand. A knowledgeable and passionate tobacconist is our best and strongest ally.

Today, with the prevalence of the Internet, blogs, and numerous publications, there is a continuous flow of accessible information. Consumers are more educated than ever, and have come to expect more. Valuable information is still generated daily at the point of sale, and is not easy to replicate. Like consumers, tobacconists are also thirsty for information and are much more knowledgeable than ever. The tobacconist's ability to understand and communicate with customers has been a vital part of taking this industry to where it is today.

In 2009 Padrón Cigars will be celebrating its 45th Anniversary. Achieving this milestone has not been easy. It has been a long and difficult journey with many obstacles. We managed to overcome past obstacles and are prepared to face future ones while remaining true to the basic principle with which my father started our company—respecting our family name by maintaining the integrity of our product.

In 2006, against my father's wishes, I shared what was until then a private part of the history of my family and our company. It was the story of "*el martillito,*" the little hammer. This is the story of how my father, a recently-arrived Cuban refugee with no money, but some carpentry skills and the willingness to work, earned a living and made his way in his new country. Working with the little hammer, the $600 he managed to save allowed him to open Padrón Cigars. It was important to share his personal experience with those who have helped us along the way; the loyal customers of Padrón Cigars. The hammer serves as a reminder of our humble origins and the importance of earning and keeping the respect of those who enjoy our cigars. It takes years of consistently great cigars to build loyal customers, but it only takes a few bad cigar experiences to lose them. Tobacconists are the last step in the long process which begins in the tobacco fields and ends with the smoker. A tobacconist's knowledge, passion, and experience, or lack of it, can make or break a truly great cigar moment.

I now look forward to the continued development of our industry. We should all understand the importance that respect for tradition and heritage has played in getting us to where we are today and where we will be in the future.

INTRODUCTION

Tobacconist: *An expert dealer in tobacco and the related accoutrements.*

T he word tobacconist can refer to an individual or a store. Tobacconist University (TU) is an educational institution with the vision to build and project the credibility of the luxury tobacco industry, in order to gain cultural acceptance around the world; preserving luxury tobacco for generations to come. Our mission compels us to research, learn, and teach in order to educate, certify, and promote the most knowledgeable and honorable tobacconists and consumers. We are building tobacconist community, culture, and credibility while providing resources for tobacconists to leverage for their customers and businesses. Retail tobacconists are an integral and historic part of the society we live in. Tobacconists represent natural, traditional, and artisanal products that bring pleasure to millions of people around the world, providing them with the impetus to relax, reflect, and savor their time. Furthermore, tobacconists are typically small, family-owned businesses pursuing their passions and living their values, despite societal, legislative, and taxation pressures. In fact, retail tobacconists are quintessential freedom fighters, in the spirit of America's founding fathers—born free and pursuing happiness as defined by the individual.

While the TU perspective is shaped by retail tobacconists, there is very little difference between tobacconists and luxury tobacco consumers. In fact, tobacconists are just tobacco consumers who are lucky enough to get paid to do what they love. Ultimately, *The Tobacconist Handbook* is as much for passionate consumers as it is for professional tobacconists.

Today, centuries after the birth of the cigar industry, the business has changed a great deal, while the cigar has changed relatively little since the 1600s. Much of the entrepreneurial spirit that first transformed rustic leaves into aromatic delicacy still exists and thrives today. In fact, we are currently living in the "golden age of cigar making."

There has never been so much creativity, variety, quality, and innovation in the luxury tobacco industry, thanks, in part, to the exodus of Cuban cigar makers/farmers/rollers and over fifty years of pioneering work in the Caribbean, Central America, and beyond. In addition, we owe thanks to consumer magazines for revolutionizing the perceptions of luxury tobacco, the Premium Cigar Association (formerly IPCPR and RTDA) for supporting professional tobacconists, and Cigar Rights of America for fighting for our rights to enjoy luxury tobacco products.

The most extraordinary contribution to the luxury tobacco industry must be credited to consumers. Their passion and ability to exchange information and build community has revolutionized our industry. Today, consumers are more knowledgeable and empowered than ever before. Without them, there would be no "golden age." Ultimately, the confluence of these forces allows us to live in a very special time, which may be the pinnacle of achievement or just the beginning.

Sadly, we are also living in the "golden age of taxation, repressive legislation, and tobacco demonization." While governments and social movements have killed, mutilated, and punished tobacco lovers throughout history, contemporary challenges and oppressive government threaten our entire industry. While we live in a privileged time with regard to product quality, it is more critical now, than ever, to educate and protect those professionals who teach, share, and preserve the rich traditions of the luxury tobacco industry—tobacconists.

Retail tobacconists are the places where cigar/pipe makers, brands, and consumers meet. They provide the most necessary service to cigar and pipe consumers, a physical place to sample, enjoy, and learn about the products they love. After all, tobacco is meant to be enjoyed by all of the senses. It must be seen, heard, touched, smelled, and tasted to be fully appreciated. You can't smell a cigar through the Internet or feel a pipe in a picture. Furthermore, camaraderie and real human connections are integral to the enjoyment of luxury tobacco. In our fast-paced world, where information travels at the speed of light, what could be healthier than settling down to relax and connecting with yourself and others? These are the simple pleasures that add real value to one's life. Above all, this is what retail tobacconists provide—a place and expertise to help you savor your time.

Here we are, past the dawn of the twenty-first century, enjoying the most extraordinary products and customers the world has ever known. Yet, we are threatened with oppression and extinction. It's a terrible irony. Rather than be hopeless, we are hopeful and filled with a sense of appreciation and purpose. While we do not expect the rest of society to pick up a cigar or pipe and enjoy it, we do hope to create a culture that can respect our traditions, taste, and values, just as we respect theirs. If you agree with this vision, then communicate your values with your legislators and please join the Cigar Rights of America and help us fight for our future. Ultimately, TU exists to share the natural artistry, magic, and wonder of luxury tobacco with consumers, tobacconists, and, more importantly, the rest of the world. We hope that our industry and customers can live in peace, relax, and know that luxury tobacco will be respected and preserved for generations to come.

As you read through this handbook, please know that it is only a distillation of the knowledge and educational materials available to you at tobacconistuniversity.org. Our entire academic curriculum, including four colleges, FAQ, glossary, hours of video, Certified Cigar Reviews, and enhanced content is available to you, for free, through our website. Please take the time to learn, share your passions, teach others, and let us know if we can add anything to improve our curriculum and your experience.

EDUCATION

"Only the educated are free." —Epictetus
"Knowledge is power." —Sir Francis Bacon

Great and learned cigar makers say that everything "depends" on the weather, sun, time, technique, etc. In fact, there is very little "black and white" or absolute certainty when it comes to luxury tobacco; even taste is subjective. No person or institution can claim to know it all or have a monopoly on knowledge. In order to compensate for these challenges, we tend to teach general concepts and then follow through with technical information on specific topics like seed varietals and rolling techniques. But, we can never teach it all since we cannot know it all. At best, education is credible information with perspective, which is what TU strives to provide.

> **TOBACCONIST TIP:**
> Taste is subjective. The "best" cigar or pipe in the world is your favorite.

We know that every leaf in a premium cigar has been touched several hundred times by human hands. Additionally, thousands of years of human intelligence, skill, and artistry goes into every cigar we smoke. The amount of knowledge needed to produce a great premium cigar is staggering. It is beyond words. Most of it must be passed down from one generation to another through human interaction and hands-on learning. The same can be said for great pipe making and any kind of luxury tobacco agriculture and blending.

The fact that premium and luxury tobacco products exist is practically a miracle. Our beloved products have been refined over thousands of years, bred and hybridized to suit our taste, grown and flourished despite weather and disease, cured and fermented with artistic care, aged to perfection, and crafted into extraordinary shapes and forms, all to be combusted and enjoyed by the ultimate consumer, destined to return to dust . . . a miracle indeed.

Great tobacconists, cigar and pipe makers, and passionate consumers never stop learning because the truth about luxury tobacco is beyond our ability to grasp. But, the magic, romance, pleasure, and camaraderie are endless and precious. Through education, we hope to enhance your appreciation and help you savor your time.

CERTIFICATION

Tobacconist University (TU) Certification is based on acceptance of the Code of Ethics and Standards and passing the final exam. TU Certification is an objective measure of knowledge, perspective, and commitment to professionalism. While there are many great tobacconists in the world, TU Certified Tobacconists have gone to extraordinary lengths to prove it. All TU Certification standards and our academic curriculum are available on our website for the world to see, use, and appreciate.

TOBACCONIST TIP:
Anybody can say they are a sommelier, certified, or master at something, but these are empty words and titles without verifiable standards. Beware of self-appointed gurus and legends in your pursuit of knowledge: always verify credentials and facts.

TU Certifications

CCT: Certified Consumer Tobacconist, a non-professional consumer degree.

CCST: Certified Cigar Sommelier Tobacconist, professional degree and designation.

CRT: Certified Retail Tobacconist, professional degree and designation.

CST: Certified Salesforce Tobacconist, professional degree and designation.

CMT: Certified Master Tobacconist, advanced professional degree and designation. A CMT must first become a CRT or CST, then complete 100 hours of apprenticeship in the field and factory and make an approved academic contribution to TU.

> **TOBACCONIST TIP:**
> CCT is the designation for Certified Consumer Tobacconists. While not a professional designation, CCT are some of the most accomplished and knowledgeable luxury tobacco consumers in the world.

CRT Code of Ethics & Standards

All Certified Tobacconists commit to the Tobacconist University Code of Ethics and Standards. As professionals, we fulfill and uphold:

Obey and enforce all local, state and federal laws regarding tobacco age/use restrictions.

Successful completion of the academic curriculum

Including Tobacco, Accoutrements, Taste and Service Colleges, the FAQ, Glossary, e-seminars, and the final exam.

Commitment to Perpetual Product Education

The brighter you are, the more you have to learn.

Customer Commitment

Tobacconist's Credo, duty, aspiration, individual attention, ambiance, courtesy, kindness, and professionalism.

Trust

Trust is the cornerstone of tobacconist credibility.

Respect & Fairness

Treat colleagues, vendors, and customers with respect, fairness, and good faith.

Merchandise all luxury tobacco products

With the same care and respect it took to create them.

Duty to package and protect all products for customers.

Finally, we are committed to be the most professional and educated ambassadors for this venerable industry and its traditions.

HISTORY—TIMELINE

Pre-Columbian

The smoking of tobacco and other leaves in the Americas has been evidenced through seven-thousand-year-old stone pipes found in southern Patagonia. Evidence also shows that the Mayan civilization in Mexico was using pipes to smoke in around 100 A.D.

1492

Christopher Columbus finds tobacco in Cuba. The indigenous Indians were rolling up tobacco leaves, inserting them into their noses (according to some accounts), and breathing out smoke.

It is widely accepted that the Arawak Indians emigrated from the mainland of South America to Cuba and brought the original tobacco seeds with them. By the early 1500s, the Tainos, Cuban natives descended from the Arawaks, had already shown Spaniards their intricate and laborious processes for growing and processing tobacco. The steps of transplanting seedlings, creating *pilones* for *fermentations*, and even packaging and aging leaves in palm bark remain the foundations of cigar production today.

1500s

France, England, and Holland begin using snuff and smoking tobacco in pipes.

1518

Conquistador Hernan Cortez brings tobacco seeds back to King Charles V of Spain.

1520

Having developed a taste for the plant, Spanish settlers in Cuba begin to cultivate tobacco for personal use.

TOBACCONIST TIP:
Over the centuries, and long before the twenty-first century, taxation, imprisonment, spiritual condemnation, and physical mutilation were all used as punishment for tobacco users.

1602

Pipe smoking has spread throughout Europe and reached parts of China, India, and Japan.

1612

Settlers begin to cultivate tobacco in Jamestown, Virginia. John Rolfe (husband of Princess Pocahontas) is the first settler to grow tobacco commercially for export.

1629

France's Cardinal Richelieu levies a tax of thirty sols on a pound of tobacco. This trend toward taxation spreads throughout Europe as tobacco usage becomes impossible to stop.

1676

The cigar, as we know it today (wrapper, binder, filler), is born in Sevilla, Spain, where thousands of laborers give birth to the cigar industry.

1700s

Cigar factories sprout up across Europe, including Rome, Germany, and France.

1717

King Felipe V of Spain organizes a monopoly on the cultivation of tobacco in Cuba. Cubans will be relegated to supplying raw tobacco for the "mother" country for the next hundred years instead of developing their own cigar industry. For taxation and control purposes, cigar production in Cuba remains illegal until 1817.

1750s

Meerschaum, found in central Europe, is discovered to be an excellent material for pipe bowls.

1798

Lithography, a color printing process, is invented, sparking marketing and advertising advancements through printed cigar labels.

1817

King Ferdinand VII, by royal decree, makes the production and sale of tobacco a legal endeavor in Cuba, sparking the birth of the Cuban cigar industry.

1827

Don Jaime Partagas establishes *Flor de Tabacos Partagas y Companía* on the edge of Old Havana, where it still operates today.

1830s

Cuban archives indicate the use of cigar bands.

1836

Chromolithography is invented in Germany and later perfected in the United States by the creator of the first greeting card, Louis Prang. Chromolithography is the use of more than one color and stone (up to twenty-five stones).

1840 (circa)

Francois Comoy begins carving pipes out of briar in Saint-Claude, France. Briar was a revolutionary material because it enabled smokers to hold the bowl in their hand, which was impossible to do with clay pipes. Additionally, briar possessed a natural beauty and grain that clay did not.

1850s

The French begin producing wooden pipes with porcelain and clay bowl liners, a style of pipe that is still made today.

1850

Innovative Dutch merchant, Gustave Bock, distinguishes his own cigars by placing a paper band on them.

1859

Cuban tobacco production doubles since deregulation. Approximately thirteen hundred handmade cigar factories are in existence in and around Havana.

1868

Henry Tibbe founds The Missouri Meerschaum Company (USA), which is still the largest producer of Corncob pipes in the world.

1895

Cuban leader of independence, Jose Marti, incites revolution against Spain by sending the message of insurrection from the US to Cuba rolled in a cigar.

1905

Over seventy thousand small cigar factories are registered with the US government (maybe another thirty thousand unregistered). Seven out of ten men smoke cigars in the United States.

1920s

The cigar rolling machine is introduced in America just as Cuban cigar making is reaching the pinnacle of achievement.

The "golden era of cigar labels" winds down with the growing popularity of photomechanical printing.

Pipe smoking begins catching on in America as a sophisticated pastime. Until now, pipe shops were virtually non-existent in the US because tobacconists were primarily focused on cigars.

1929

Increasing cigarette consumption (due to industrialization), the advent of the cigar rolling machine, WWI, and the financial crash of 1929 all contribute to a substantially negative impact on the Cuban cigar industry. In addition, industrialization affects the pace of life, creating less time for the enjoyment of cigars.

1950s

In America, pipe smoking becomes the symbol of sophistication and a reassuring cultural icon, thanks in part to movies, magazines, and marketing.

1954

The Sommelier Society of America opens its doors in the United States and begins educating wine enthusiasts.

1959

Fidel Castro and the Cuban Revolution instigate a mass exodus of Cuban cigar makers to the Canary Islands, Dominican Republic, Central America, and the United States.

1960

Cuba quickly changes course and rereleases old cigar brands. The Castro government begins the process of nationalizing privately owned tobacco farms. Great cigar makers like Cifuentes, Toraño, Menendez, and Palicio were forced into exile.

1966

Birth of the famous Cuban Cohiba brand, which was created for Fidel Castro and later given away to VIPs and diplomats.

1982

The Cuban Cohiba brand is made available for sale to the public.

1992

The launching of *Cigar Aficionado* magazine by Marvin R. Shanken (publisher of *Wine Spectator*) helps instigate the beginning of a worldwide "Cigar Renaissance."

1994

The Cuban government creates Habanos S.A., which is in charge of global distribution and marketing for Cuban cigars.

1998
Commercial introduction of the Cuban Trinidad brand. Production on the Trinidad brand started in 1980 exclusively for Fidel Castro. The brand was created to take the place of the Cohiba as Cuba's most exclusive and prestigious cigar.

1999
Swedish Match, Europe's largest tobacco conglomerate, purchases the machine-made tobacco business from General Cigar, the US maker of Macanudo. SEITA S.A., the French tobacco monopoly, buys US-based Consolidated Cigar, maker of non-Cuban H. Upmann, Montecristo, Romeo y Julieta, San Luis Rey, and other famous premium brands. Later that year, SEITA S.A. merges with Spanish tobacco monopoly Tabacalera S.A. to form Altadis, the largest buyer of Cuban tobacco in the world. (Consolidated Cigar becomes Altadis, USA.)

2000
Altadis completes 50 percent acquisition ($500 million) of Habanos S.A., the global marketing and distribution division for Cuban cigars. Habanos has few physical assets, including ownership of Cuban brand names, an equity interest in Habanos retail stores around the world, and exclusive rights to distribute Cuban cigars.

2000
Swedish Match purchases 64 percent of General Cigar.

2005
Swedish Match finalizes 100 percent purchase of General Cigar.

2007
Scandinavian Tobacco Group (STG) purchases CAO. Swedish Match purchases online retailer Cigars International.

2009
STG purchases factories that produce Torano brands and begins merger with Swedish Match, taking a 51 percent stake in the new company.

2011
On April 15, the Traditional Cigar Manufacturing and Small Business Jobs Preservation Act (H.R. 1639) is introduced in the US House of Representatives calling for regulatory exemption for narrowly defined class of premium cigars. This is the first time the industry has initiated such legislative protection.

2014
In April, the FDA releases the Proposed Rule to begin regulating e-cigarettes, cigars, and pipe tobaccos. The proposed regulations could make the introduction of new cigar and pipe tobacco products economically impossible.

2014
Swisher International, one of the world's largest machine made cigar makers, buys Drew Estate, the largest manufacturer of premium infused/flavored cigars.

2015
Imperial Tobacco creates Tabacalera USA to oversee Altadis USA, JR Cigar, and Casa de Montecristo, continuing the trend of

vertically integrated companies controlling productions, retail and mail order: direct, from seed to consumer.

2016

On May 10, the FDA publishes the Final Rule deeming all tobacco products subject to its authority. Part of this rule outlaws all products not manufactured/marketed before February 15, 2007, unless approved by the FDA. On July 15, a lawsuit is filed by CRA, IPCPR (PCA), and CAA to combat the onerous regulatory agenda of the FDA.

2017

On December 14, the CRA, IPCPR (PCA), and CAA lawsuit oral arguments are made. This is the first time the industry is in court to litigate the federal regulation of the industry.

2017

Swedish Match sells off all their interests in the cigar industry. Altria Group, Inc. (parent company of Philip Morris) purchases Nat Sherman, including their cigar brands, the NYC Townhouse flagship retail location, and cigarette brand portfolio.

2018

FDA Commissioner Dr. Scott Gottlieb announces ANPRM (Advance Notice of Proposed Rule Making) in speech calling for new public comment on premium cigars while Federal Judge Amit Mehta delays warning labels on cigar boxes.

2019

On April 5, US Senator Marco Rubio has first ever congressional hearing exclusively on issue of premium cigar regulation. By September, national media outlets in the US report on more than 450 cases of mysterious lung illnesses and a handful of deaths linked to vaping. The FDA announces its intention to ban flavored e-cigarettes.

2020

The saga continues. Business and brand consolidations continue in the cigar and pipe tobacco industry as the culture war against smokers and regulatory threats continue to grow. Taxation and denormalization of smokers is reaching new heights, which threatens the industry, consumers, and basic freedoms.

NICOTIANA TABACUM

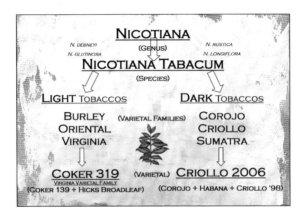

Tobacco refers to *Nicotiana tabacum*, one of over sixty species in the botanical genus *Nicotiana*. The original *N. tabacum* strain has never been found growing in the wild; yet, its descendant varietals are the most widely grown non-food crop plant (species) on Earth.

Within the *N. tabacum* species, there are two general classifications for tobacco: **light** and **dark**. Light tobaccos are used for cigarettes and pipe tobaccos. Dark tobaccos are typically used for cigar tobaccos. Under these general classifications, there are also varietal families of tobacco like Burley, Oriental, and Virginia, which are all light tobaccos. Two of the more famous dark varietal families are **Corojo** and **Criollo** (see next section). Each of these varietal families started as a unique seed strain and has since been hybridized and distilled into other varietals. In the case of Corojo and Criollo, the original varietals are still being grown, but derivative varietals are far more common—they have expanded into a family with many descendants, but they are all tobacco.

While all of the known varietals of tobacco have resulted from some form of hybridization and/or natural selection, the differences in plant structure, taste+aroma characteristics, quality, and end-use are astounding. Cigarettes, cigars, pipe tobaccos, and snuff all require different varietals, which will be grown, cured, and processed in completely different ways.

Particularly notable with cigar and pipe tobaccos is the extreme skill and attention required to make it delicious—an extraordinary **organoleptic** delicacy. Growing great tobacco is less like traditional agriculture (growing potatoes) and more like artisanal horticulture (breeding and raising rare orchids): it is extremely time, labor, capital, and intellectually intensive. Another unique characteristic of tobacco is the way we use the leaves of the plant instead of its fruit or flowers. Tobacco is indubitably the planet's most unique and valued crop plant.

> **TOBACCONIST TIP:**
> The term flavor refers to the combination of taste and aroma. Throughout this book and the TU academic curriculum, we use the term "taste+aroma" to emphasize the importance and synergy of the two senses.

CIGAR TOBACCO

Cigar Varietals

While there are too many dark (*air-cured*) tobacco varietals to discuss in detail, there are a handful of families that consumers and tobacconists should be familiar with. For more details, see the following chapter, which covers the growing regions for cigars.

Wrappers

Famous wrapper leaf varietal families include **Broadleaf**, **Cameroon** (Central African), **Connecticut**, **Corojo**, and **Sumatra**. While many of these varietals are named after the place they were popularized, they can be grown in different countries and produce different results. For that reason, a Connecticut varietal grown in

Ecuador is called *Ecuadoran-Connecticut* and a Sumatran varietal grown in Ecuador is called *Ecuadoran-Sumatran*. Similarly, *Cuban-Corojo* will produce a different result than *Nicaraguan-Corojo*, so they deserve a different name.

> **TOBACCONIST TIP:**
> Binder leaves can come from either wrapper or filler plants. A marred wrapper leaf can be used as binder while a strong filler leaf with the necessary burn characteristics can also be used as a binder.

Filler

A few of the world's most popular filler leaf varietal families are *Criollo*, *Olor Dominicano*, and *Piloto Cubano*. While these varietal families have many descendants, they are usually referred to by their family name, with no more specificity given. But, as we are learning, a *Cuban-Criollo* will be very different from a *Honduran-Criollo*. Most of the initial differences will result from the specific microclimate, but, over time, seed strains and plants grown in a particular cigar region will begin to take on more distinctive characteristics.

Although all of these varietals or their forefathers originated in Cuba, they are given new names when they begin to distinguish themselves in a new region. In the absence of any international standards, cigar manufacturers and marketers do not have to follow any guidelines when declaring and naming the varietals they grow or the leaves that go into a particular cigar. In fact, many happen to like

> **TOBACCONIST TIP:**
> The *Criollo 2006* varietal is a hybrid of *Corojo*, *Habana*, and *Criollo '98*. As you can see, dark air-cured tobacco varietal hybrids can get complex.

it this way so they can keep their prized ingredients a secret, while divulging only general information.

Varietal vs. Varietal Family

Understanding tobacco at the individual varietal level is so complex that many cigar makers spend their lifetimes perfecting their knowledge and techniques. This level of nuance and knowledge can be too specific for consumers and tobacconists. Instead, over the last couple chapters, we have focused on studying and understanding tobaccos at the more general varietal family level. The next chapter, Cigar Growing Regions, will have more specific information about the unique varietals being grown in different parts of the world. But, a thorough education would not be complete without an in-depth study of at least two of the most famous seed varietals in the history of cigars: **Corojo** and **Criollo**. Their descendants are in most premium cigars made today. While many hybrids have been created over the years, both inside and outside of Cuba, these two legendary seed strains make excellent specimens for serious study.

> **TOBACCONIST TIP:**
> Luxury tobacco is defined as tobacco products that are created by master craftsmen utilizing *premium* quality tobacco and intended to be enjoyed while savoring your time. Luxury and premium tobaccos are not homogenized, commoditized, or used out of habit or addiction.

Criollo

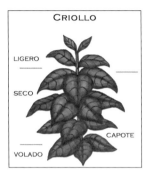

Origins date back to the time when Columbus discovered the "New World."

Traditionally used as filler and binder plant.

Criollo is grown under direct sunlight to amplify the variety and intensity of taste+aroma.

For generations, the Criollo plant produced most of the filler leaves in a "Havana" cigar.

Produces six to seven pairs of leaves and is **primed** in pairs.

Ligero: leaves at the top of the plant are the strongest and fuller flavored due to direct sunlight. Leaves toward the bottom of the plant are more subtle in flavor and strength. **Seco & Volado** leaves are used for filler. **Capote** leaves are used for binder.

> **TOBACCONIST TIP:**
> Outside of Cuba [and the *Criollo* varietal], tobacco plant leaves are generally classified, from top to bottom, as:
> **CORONA, LIGERO, VISO, SECO, and VOLADO**

Corojo

COROJO

CORONAS

CENTRO
GORDO

CENTRO
FINO

CENTRO
LIGERO

UNO Y
MEDIO

LIBRE DE
PIE

Developed in the 1930s by Diego Rodriguez.

Derived from the *Criollo* seed through selective breeding.

Named after its birthplace, the farm *Santa Ines del Corojo* in the Vuelta Abajo region of Cuba.

The premier wrapper for Cuban cigars until the 1990s.

Primarily **shade-grown** under wrappers.

Weakness: still susceptible to Blue-Mold, Black Shank, and other tobacco ravaging diseases.

Produces eight to nine pairs of leaves and is **primed** in pairs.

Praised for its dark brown (*colorado*) color, uniformity, and thin veins.

> **TOBACCONIST TIP:**
> In addition to wrapper and binder leaf, premium cigars can contain another three to six distinct filler leaves. Actually, wrapper and binder use half a plant leaf, while fillers use partial leaves.

Processing: Art & Science
Air-Curing

Curing is the process of drying tobacco while halting the maturation process, fixing the sugars in the leaf, and releasing chlorophyll. **Air-curing** is the method used to cure dark tobacco leaves, which will be used for cigars. It is a clean and natural process that prepares the leaves for their next step: **fermentation**.

During air-curing, leaves are tied in pairs, hung on lathes (*cujes*), and placed high up in a curing/drying barn for approximately fifty days. These curing barns (*Casas de Tabaco*) usually face east/west for optimal air circulation. Traditionally, *Casas de Tabaco* are made of wood framing with walls and roofs made of palm leaves. While these structures are still common, newer curing barns can be made with more modern materials, such as wood sheets or metal. These structures usually have an array of doors and vents on all sides and at varying heights to manage temperature and air circulation.

Fermentation

Fermentation is the organic process that accounts for the majority of change and distinction in cigar tobaccos. Fermentation is like a natural, slow cooking process whereby the tobacco heats up under the pressure of its own weight and moisture. Carefully controlling the temperature cycles and tobacco humidity allows the tobacco to slowly expel (or sweat out) the ammonia and impurities in the leaves. Meanwhile, the flavor (taste+aroma) qualities of the tobacco develop. Unlike alcohol fermentation, tobacco fermentation does not produce any new "side effects." Instead, it purifies the leaf and allows the taste+aroma characteristics to express themselves.

Due to the unpredictability of the raw material, there is no pure scientific way to control fermentation and achieve a desired "taste" or specific result. Fermentation is part art, science, and a natural wonder. Fermentation is where the artistry and intuition of the cigar maker will be tested the most.

> **TOBACCONIST TIP:**
> After air-curing, leaves are tied into bunches of approximately five leaves called *gavillas.* Wrapper leaves can stay in the *gavilla* bundle through the fermentation and *añejamiento* stages.

TU teaches the traditional Cuban two-stage fermentation method to illustrate the most important points.

During the **first fermentation,** the leaves are moistened and laid in one- to three-foot-tall piles called *pilones.* When the temperature reaches about 95°F, the *pilones* are unraveled and redistributed. This is done because the center of the *pilone* will always be hotter, and outer leaves must be rotated inward. This process repeats for about thirty days. Note: leaf sorting will occur before and after each fermentation; they are organized by size, type, texture, progress, color, etc.

The **second fermentation** involves piling the tobacco into *burros*, approximately four to six feet tall. It will last about sixty days and reach a maximum temperature of about 108°F. The same systematic unraveling and redistributing will occur over the course of this fermentation. The greatest danger during this vigorous fermentation is overheating the leaf and exhausting its organoleptic qualities; this can happen very quickly and within a couple of degrees.

TOBACCONIST TIP:
Originally, the Cuban *Cohiba* brand was touted as undergoing a third fermentation, at lower than usual temperatures. In reality, the third fermentation may just be a form of añejamiento.

While the length of fermentation will vary among the different types of tobaccos, heavier leaves (like *ligero*) will take longer and possibly ferment at higher temperatures. Ultimately, fermentation will expel most of the ammonia and impurities from good tobacco and develop the taste+aroma potential. Fermentation cannot make bad tobacco good, but it can ruin good tobacco. Furthermore, fermentation techniques are the key to successfully eliciting the greatest potential of any tobacco.

Maduro

In its most limited sense, the term *maduro* can simply refer to a black(ish) color of a wrapper leaf. A leaf can end up darker if it comes from a late **priming** or a **stalk-cut** plant. But, a true *maduro* cigar will have a wrapper that has undergone longer and/or more intense (higher temperature) fermentation. This "enhanced" fermentation releases the natural sugars in the leaf and yields a natural sweetness. In addition, the extra fermentation will round out the spices in the leaf and make it richer in flavor.

TOBACCONIST TIP:
Cigar leaves must be at very high humidity levels when they are rolled: between 80–95 percent.

Añejamiento

Also known as aging, *añejamiento* is the very slow, temperature- and climate-controlled process of organic decomposition. While it is not nearly as intense as fermentation, *añejamiento* is critical to the refinement of great tobaccos.

Tobacco *Añejamiento* occurs in small batches after fermentation. It can last for years, until the leaves are rolled into a cigar. While filler and binder leaves are usually wrapped in sackcloth bundles, wrapper leaves receive extra care and can be wrapped in ***tercios***.

Cigar *Añejamiento* starts after the cigar is rolled and ends when the cigar is smoked. See the Cigar Preservation chapter for more information on cigar aging.

> **TOBACCONIST TIP:**
> It is possible to skip tobacco *añejamiento* and roll a
> cigar when the leaves have stabilized after fermentation.
> However, this cigar will develop and age differently.

CIGAR GROWING REGIONS

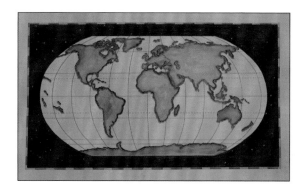

Premium cigar tobacco is a precious plant that can only be cultivated in select regions of the world where the soil, climate, topography, people, skill, and tradition converge. While tobacco is grown from Canada to New Zealand, the *best* cigar tobacco is grown between the Tropic of Cancer and the Tropic of Capricorn, along the equator. Great cigar tobaccos are grown in valleys where they benefit from *nutrient erosion, condensation irrigation,* and *sunlight manipulation.*

The following pages offer a glimpse of the amazing variety of specialized cigar tobaccos being grown around the globe. The most exciting aspect of contemporary cigar growing regions is that many places are just beginning to realize their potential. In the last half century, and more so in the last decade, there have been extraordinary developments and improvements in premium cigar cultivation. Each region we will study has specific advantages, potential, and challenges associated with it. A deeper analysis will reveal the uniqueness of each cigar growing region.

Africa
Central African Republic and Cameroon

The countries of Cameroon and the Central African Republic produce tobaccos commonly referred to as *Cameroon*, more accurately called *Central African*. Originally descended from *Sumatran* seed, today's Central African varietals are known for their rich flavors and aromas. The hearty soils in this region of Africa yield a distinctive tobacco that does not need much fertilization and is grown under direct sun. Consistent climate and cloudy conditions allow wrapper cultivation without the use of *shade cloth*. Central African tobacco lends itself to wrapper production due to its appearance, supple texture, and resilient strength. These wrappers have a luscious dark brown color, often with an attractive reddish tint. They are fuller flavored and can have a unique "toothy" or grainy texture. Traditionally, most Central African tobacco produced smaller leaves. Today, the quality and size of the leaves are making larger wrapper leaves, which makes larger cigars possible.

> **TOBACCONIST TIP:**
> Cigar tobacco plants require approximately eight hours of sunlight per day.

It is worth noting that the cigar growing regions in these countries are typically isolated within rain forests and mountainous areas. Growing tobacco in Africa is a very labor- and resource-intensive enterprise. While the French started growing and developing Central African tobacco in the 1950s, the quality was more generic or commodity-oriented, rather than luxury. Throughout the 1990s, the Meerapfel family pioneered the development of premium Central African tobacco by investing heavily in infrastructure and human resources. Due to the isolation of much of the great cigar growing areas, entire villages were built and labor forces relocated in order to produce premium tobacco. Today, the supply of Central African tobacco is much closer to meeting consumer demand because of the sacrifices, commitment, and long-term vision of these extraordinary cigar makers.

> **TOBACCONIST TIP:**
> What is a cigar maker? Literally speaking, a cigar maker is a roller (*torcedore*), or the factory owner who manages/controls roller production. But, this term is very limiting because a cigar maker can be a blender or farmer as well. When we use the term cigar maker, we are typically taking the broad view and describing any one of the artisans and experts involved in cigar cultivation and production.

Asia
Indonesia—Sumatra

The tradition of growing cigar tobacco in Indonesia, specifically on the tropical islands of Sumatra and Java, goes back hundreds of years. The rich, volcanic soils of the island produce a tobacco with color, flavor, and aroma characteristics that are between Connecticut and Central African varieties. The seed varietal grown in Indonesia is distinctive and old enough to merit its own name, Sumatra. Sumatran seed tobacco is grown extensively in Mexico and Ecuador as well. Whether grown in Sumatra or expatriated to other countries (Ecuadorian-Sumatra or Mexican-Sumatra), this tobacco is consistently dark in color, rich in flavor, not particularly complex, and produces excellent wrapper leaves.

Philippines

Located northeast of Indonesia, the Philippine islands are not especially famous for growing premium tobacco leaf, but they do produce enough mild and subtly rich tobacco to merit mention. Philippine tobacco is popular as a filler component in many small and machine-made cigars. These tobaccos are rarely found in today's premium and luxury products.

Caribbean
Cuba

Cuba is the birthplace of premium cigar tobacco. The agricultural, curing, and fermentation traditions that are used throughout the world today were first developed in Cuba. The best tobacco growing area in Cuba lies in the western part of the island in the Pinar del Rio province and within the Vuelta Abajo region of that province. Excellent tobacco is also grown in the central region of Cuba. Cuban tobacco is famous for its robust flavor, fuller body, and spicy aromas. The unique microclimate and soil of Cuba creates supple and strong leaves, which can be exquisite in appearance, flavor, and aroma.

> **TOBACCONIST TIP:**
> The Vuelta Abajo valley in the Pinar del Rio province of Cuba is considered the most famous cigar growing region in the world. It gets around sixty-five inches of rainfall per year, yet only two of those inches fall during the growing season. **Condensation irrigation** and mechanical irrigation methods can be used to supplement water during the growing season.

Dominican Republic

Known in the trade as "the DR," this island neighbor of Cuba has become one of the world's most exquisite tobacco growing regions. Thanks, in part, to an indigenous tobacco culture and many years of painstaking investment and labor, the DR is easily one of the premier cigar tobacco growing regions in the world today. Historically, the DR produced relatively mild filler tobaccos, but the last two decades have seen this country develop fuller and heavier bodied tobaccos and wrapper leaf.

The two main families of tobacco grown in the DR are *Olor Dominicano* and *Piloto Cubano*. *Olor Dominicano* is the family of tobacco that is indigenous to the Dominican Republic, and it produces a thinner and less substantive leaf than *Piloto*. *Olor* tobaccos are prized for their complex aromas and excellent burning and blending qualities. *Piloto* plants grown in the DR tend to be fuller bodied and more resilient than their *Olor* counterparts.

The main growing region in the Dominican Republic centers around the city of Santiago, which is in the northern part of the country. Nestled in the Cibao River Valley between two mountain ranges, the soil, people, and conditions in this area can produce an amazing array of quality tobacco.

Jamaica

While there are indigenous and wild forms of *Nicotiana* (Cow Tongue/Silver Tongue) growing throughout this island nation, there was never a deeply rooted cigar culture in Jamaica. Around 1875, Cuban émigrés brought tobacco seeds to Jamaica and started the local cigar industry. Over the last century, many popular brands have used Jamaican tobacco as part of their filler blends. There have also been a number of very famous brands, including Royal Jamaica and Macanudo, rolled there as well. For a multitude of reasons, including war, hurricanes, and labor problems, the island has failed to achieve the status and momentum of neighboring Cuba and the Dominican Republic. The final chapter on Jamaican tobacco has yet to be written.

Puerto Rico

Puerto Rico has been growing and producing premium cigars for hundreds of years. Puerto Rican cigar tobacco is *sun-grown,* relatively mild in taste, and has good burning qualities. This relatively unexciting description, coupled with higher local production costs, is why Puerto Rican tobacco remains relatively obscure in the premium cigar marketplace.

Central America
Costa Rica

Known for its extraordinary ecosystems, volcanoes, and tropical forests, Costa Rica has emerged as a boutique grower of premium cigar leaf over the last decade. While the country produces some premium filler and binder tobacco, dark and *maduro* wrapper leaf from Costa Rica is becoming a popular substitute for Brazilian, Mexican, and Broadleaf varietals.

> **TOBACCONIST TIP:**
> The greatest cigar tobacco growing regions are found in valleys. The topography of valleys provides the benefit of **nutrient erosion** and **condensation irrigation.**

Honduras

While Honduras is home to its own wild variety of *Nicotiana*, *Copaneco*, it is also regarded as an ideal place to grow Cuban and Connecticut seed varietals for premium cigars. In the southeastern part of Honduras, just north of the Nicaraguan border, lies the most significant premium cigar tobacco producing region in the country, the town of Danli and the Jamastran Valley, both in the province of El Paraiso. These areas are the epicenter of cigar production and a primary growing region for the country's best tobacco. Since the 1960s, cigar makers have been likening the Jamastran

Valley to Pinar del Rio, and, judging from the full-bodied tobacco they grow, there are many similarities. Today, Connecticut shade-grown and Corojo shade-grown tobaccos are cultivated extensively throughout the region. Additionally, Honduras also produces very large amounts of Cuban seed sun-grown filler tobaccos, which are found in hundreds of brands today. Honduran premium cigar tobacco production is of high quality, dynamic, and consistently improving.

> **TOBACCONIST TIP:**
> John Rolfe was the first colonist to cultivate tobacco commercially in Jamestown (VA) in 1612. It was so economically successful that incentives had to be created to encourage colonists to grow food.

Mexico

In the San Andreas Valley, southeast of the port city Veracruz, nestled between volcanoes and a large lake, is the heart of Mexican cigar country. While some Mexican cigars have had a less-than-spectacular reputation, it belies the fact that many premium and famous brands use Mexican fillers and wrappers in their blends. Soil in the San Andreas Valley is extraordinarily rich and produces a distinctive tasting tobacco. Until 1996, when tobacco import duties were dropped, Mexico produced primarily *puros*, which consumers either loved or hated. Regardless of personal preference, Mexican tobaccos are distinctive and fill a special niche in the marketplace. The most famous of Mexican cigar tobaccos is San Andreas Negro. Like Connecticut Broadleaf, San Andreas Negro was traditionally **stalk-cut** and lends itself to binder and maduro wrapper production. This varietal is a tough leaf that can withstand the extra fermentation required to produce a maduro. Other varietals, such as

Mexican-Sumatra, are also successfully grown in the San Andreas Valley.

> **TOBACCONIST TIP:**
> Cigar making is a high risk, laborious, and capital-intensive business. Even under perfect conditions, it takes years for a seed to evolve into a cigar. Weather, disease, political, labor, and time factors heavily impact the cigar making process.

Nicaragua

Since the 1960s, Nicaragua has had many political difficulties that disrupted and inhibited cigar tobacco production. But, over the last decade, Nicaragua has proven itself capable of producing some of the most rich, spicy, aromatic, and complex tobacco in the world. In the northern part of the country, not far from the Honduran border, are the towns of Esteli and Condega. Esteli is home to the majority of Nicaraguan cigar production, but both towns are surrounded by volcanic soil and fertile land that produces lush fields of Cuban seed tobacco. Northeast of Esteli and Condega lies the Jalapa Valley. Like so many locations in the world of cigars, Jalapa is remote and diffi-cult to get to, but the land is fertile and produces tobacco of extraor-dinary quality. If the last decade is an indication of the potential for Nicaraguan cigar tobacco, then our palates have reason to be excited.

> **TOBACCONIST TIP:**
> Leather cigar cases are **hygroscopic,** so they can dehydrate or absorb moisture from a well-conditioned cigar. While elegant, these cases should be used as a short-term solution—for an evening out or less than a day.

North America
Connecticut River Valley

There are two distinctive cigar varietals being grown in this unexpected North American location: Connecticut Shade and Connecticut Broadleaf. Just north of Harford, Connecticut, lies an amazing cigar growing area known as the Connecticut River Valley. The term "Connecticut" is not limited to the state, but refers to the river valley that runs through Massachusetts. The soil in this valley is of glacial origins, which means it was deposited after the last ice age. It is less robust than volcanic soil and produces a distinctive and light flavored tobacco.

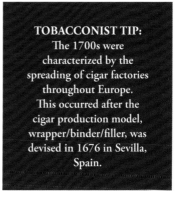

TOBACCONIST TIP:
The 1700s were characterized by the spreading of cigar factories throughout Europe. This occurred after the cigar production model, wrapper/binder/filler, was devised in 1676 in Sevilla, Spain.

Connecticut Shade

In 1900, a Cuban seed varietal was brought to the valley in an attempt to simulate the Sumatra seed wrapper tobacco that was already being imported into the country. Sumatra seed grown in the valley gave poor results, but the Cuban seed, grown under shade with muslin or cheesecloth, successfully gave birth to Connecticut shade-grown wrapper. Due to its northern location, the growing season in Connecticut is earlier in the year, between May and September. The plants are tall and elegant, reaching heights of over ten feet. Today, Connecticut Shade, as it is called, is one of the world's most prized and beautiful wrapper leaves. It has extraordinary strength, small veins, silky texture, and consistent light tan to golden brown color.

> **TOBACCONIST TIP:**
> All wrapper leaves have their center stem completely removed, but filler leaves only have half. After the stem is removed from a wrapper leaf, there are two remaining halves that are mirror images of each other. Each half of the leaf will wrap one cigar—sometimes two cigars if it is large enough. The bottom, veiny side of the leaf will face inward, touching the binder. While the smoother, top side of the leaf will be outside of the cigar. The shape of the half-leaf, coupled with the smooth side needing to face outward, means that cigars get rolled both right-to-left and left-to-right. Hence, cigar wrapping/rolling is an "ambidextrous" art!

Connecticut Broadleaf

While Connecticut Shade is tall, elegant, smooth, and silky, its counterpart, the Connecticut Broadleaf plant, is small with enormous leaves. Broadleaf varietals can be grown next to Connecticut Shade, but must be directly under the sun. They are **stalk-cut** instead of being **primed** like shade-grown plants and require more fermentation than their shade-grown neighbors.

Connecticut Broadleaf tobacco is a dense and oily tobacco that darkens easily and is commonly used on maduro cigars as a wrapper. Over the last century, Broadleaf has been a popular wrapper for many mass-market cigars, but, with extra care and fermentation, it yields excellent wrappers for premium cigars. Connecticut Broadleaf grows a little thicker, rougher, and oilier than Mexican Broadleaf.

> **TOBACCONIST TIP:**
> Any tobacco leaf used as a cigar wrapper must be elastic, have high tensile strength, consistent color, and texture. Wrapper leaves must be as resilient as they are beautiful. These stringent criteria make wrapper leaves the most expensive part of a cigar.

South America
Brazil

Tobacco has probably been smoked in Brazil in pipe or cigar form almost as long as tobacco has been smoked by humans. Most Brazilian tobacco is produced for domestic and European cigarettes and machine-made cigars. Premium cigar tobacco did not gain momentum in Brazil until the 1960s. Brazilian cigar tobacco occupies an important niche in the wrapper market and is emerging as a popular filler tobacco as well.

In the eastern province of Bahia, there is a small swath of land less than two hundred miles across called the Reconcavo Basin. It is bordered to the east by the Bay of All Saints and then the Atlantic Ocean. The Reconcavo Basin produces a distinctive wrapper tobacco called *Mata Fina* and its lesser cousins *Mata Sul* and *Mata Norte* (stronger). *Mata Fina* is a sun-grown tobacco that is typically made into wrappers. It has a dark color, mild to medium strength, rich flavor, is very aromatic, and has a natural sweetness that yields excellent *Oscuro* and *Maduro* colored wrappers.

> **TOBACCONIST TIP:**
> Stalk-priming is the process of harvesting approximately a pair of leaves per week, but starts at the top and works down the plant. In addition, leaves are picked with a small piece of the stalk intact, holding the leaf pairs together.

Colombia

The thought that Colombia produces premium cigar tobacco surprises a lot of people. Historically speaking, Colombian cigar tobacco varietals (Carmen, Ovjas, Zambrano, and Plate) have had a reputation for being tough, thick, and requiring heavy fermentation. Contemporary cigar blenders are searching to find a distinctive filler tobacco that will balance and set their brand apart. More than a few modern brands are currently using Colombian fillers to accomplish that goal. Current use of Colombian tobacco is an excellent example of how cigar blenders and growers push the limits of luxury tobacco to create and discover new delicacies and possibilities. The future looks bright for premium Colombian cigar tobacco.

> **TOBACCONIST TIP:**
> While seven out of ten men smoked cigars around 1905, by the 1920s, a decline in premium cigar smoking was precipitated by the advent of the cigar rolling machine, the financial crash of 1929, and the mass production of cigarettes. Ultimately, industrialization quickened the pace of life and led to the shift from cigars to cigarettes.

Ecuador

Located on the northwestern coast of South America, Ecuador has been growing premium cigar filler and wrappers since the 1960s. Its unique location provides Ecuadorian-grown tobacco with consistent cloud cover throughout the growing season. Ecuadorian wrappers are said to be **cloud-grown** instead of **shade-grown**. This naturally diffused light diminishes vein size, yields thinner leaves, and creates a supple leaf with consistent color. Ecuador is famous for having over thirty volcanoes and extremely rich volcanic soil. In Ecuador, most tobacco is grown in the foothills of the Andean mountains. The greatest threat to Ecuadorian tobacco is the *El Niño* effect. When the Pacific waters warm up, tremendous amounts of rain are unleashed in Ecuador, which makes tobacco cultivation impossible.

The two most popular seed varietals grown in Ecuador are Connecticut and Sumatran. Both Ecuadorian-Sumatra and Ecuadorian-Connecticut plants exhibit milder strength and flavor when grown in Ecuador, perhaps due to the unique cloudiness or different soil. Ecuadorian-Connecticut plants can grow over ten feet tall while their Ecuadorian-Sumatran counterparts mature at approximately six feet.

Peru

While this Andean nation does not have a long tradition of growing premium cigar tobacco, it does have some ideal growing areas. Currently, some famous brands are using Peruvian filler leaf as distinctive (taste+aroma) component in their blends. As long as cigar makers seek new ways to differentiate their blends, the future for Peruvian tobacco seems bright.

Venezuela

Similar to Colombia, there is a recent trend developing for premium cigar tobacco in Venezuela. While the country has cigar traditions going back hundreds of years, it has the potential to emerge as a viable premium filler producer for the world market.

TOBACCONIST TIP:
The Cuban Revolution of 1959 instigated a mass exodus of cigar makers to the Dominican Republic, Canary Islands, Central America, and the United States of America. This "brain drain" helped usher in the "golden age of cigar making" that is occurring today, albeit decades later.

SEED TO CIGAR

The tobacco flower. The best plants are allowed to develop their flowers for seed harvesting. This helps select stronger and better subsequent generations.

Specially selected flowers/seed pods are dried and harvested for seeds. Each pod yields dozens of seeds for future generations.

Semilleros are protected greenhouses where tobacco seedlings are allowed to germinate. Approximately one ounce of tobacco seeds equals three hundred thousand seeds; they are tiny, almost grain-like.

Seedlings will stay in the semilleros between one to two months and then be transplanted to the fields. The young plants are inspected and pruned to strengthen stalk and root growth.

Semillero grown seedlings are planted in individual soil pods to protect the roots and for easy transplanting to the fields.

Seedlings are transplanted to the field (in this case, a **shade-grown** field). After transplanting, it will take a couple of weeks for the plants to adapt, perk up, and start growing. Notice the precise layout.

Cigar tobacco plants require a perfect balance of water; too much water will cause them to drown or rot. Here, you can see the process of canal irrigation and a laborer directing water to the plants by hand.

This photo shows a crop of Criollo '98 in the DR about thirty days after transplanting. Dominican tobaccos take approximately 90–110 days to reach maturity; these have over one month to go.

Whether sun or shade-grown, all cigar tobacco plants are visited daily to check for parasites and fungi. In addition, smaller and underdeveloped leaves will be pruned off; this is called **deshijando**.

Notice the cheesecloth that is draped over **shade-grown** wrapper plants. Some larger plant varietals must be tied to the cloth structure so the plants will grow up straight.

Good genetics and the extra care and effort applied in the semi-lleros will produce consistent crops like the one pictured here in the Jamastran Valley of Honduras.

Spray irrigation can be used to water cigar tobacco plants, as is shown with this crop of *Piloto Cubano* in Jalapa, Nicaragua.

Maturing cigar tobacco plants can begin to dwarf the people that work with them. This field in Jalapa, Nicaragua, is almost ready for **priming**.

The flowers in this picture have been preserved and marked with a red string. They will be harvested, and their seeds will be used for future generations. The leaves from these plants will not be used in cigars.

The **topping** process means the flower buds will be removed before they bloom. This will keep nutrients and energy flowing to the leaves instead of the flower.

As these plants mature, you will notice the enormous, body-builder-like veins bringing nutrients to every leaf. At maturity, the leaves will begin to lay flat and the center vein will begin to turn yellow.

The cigar tobacco harvest process is called **priming**. It begins by picking two to three leaves from the bottom of every plant about once a week. Notice how delicately the leaves must be handled.

During the harvest/priming, the only machines used are the vehicles that carry the tobacco to the curing barns. Everything else is done by hand.

After priming, leaves are tied or sewn together in pairs and hung on lathes, also known as **cujes**.

The cujes are raised high into the *casa de tabaco* to begin the **air-curing** process.

As the cigar tobacco begins to dry, it will break down the chlorophyll and begin to turn from green to yellow to brown. The entire process can take almost two months.

Air-curing involves rotating the cujes, over time, from the top of the barn towards the bottom. In some cases, very small fires can be lit in the barns to control high moisture levels and temperature.

Fermentation, which can last months, will slowly release ammonia and impurities from the tobacco as the taste+aroma qualities begin to develop. The pilones, or burros, will heat up under their own weight.

The paper tags you see above help keep track of the tobacco types and fermentation procedures, including when and at what temperature the piles are unraveled and reassembled.

The long process of aging, called **tobacco** *añejamiento*, starts after the fermentations. All leaf types will be aged separately, with *ligeros* taking the longest.

Sorting by quality, type, and size occurs before, after, and sometimes during *añejamiento*. In fact, there is always some kind of sorting going on throughout the cigar making process.

A day before leaves get rolled into cigars, they must be re-humidified—this process is called **mojo**. The mojo is particularly important and delicate for wrappers, which will be stretched when applied.

Wrapper leaves will have their center stem removed so each half of the leaf can be applied to an individual cigar. Some cigar makers will use a machine to assist the process, but agile hands are still necessary.

Wrapper leaves go through another sorting process to make sure shades and sizes are properly allocated. Notice the need for water to keep the leaf pliable.

Blending requires a master blender to allocate the "recipe" of a particular cigar to the rollers. The recipe consists of precisely measured amounts of specific fillers, binder, and wrapper leaves.

Cigar rollers combine three to five filler leaves and wrap them with a binder leaf—this process is called **bunching**. At this point, extreme skill is required to create a cigar that will burn and draw perfectly.

The bunch, or *enpuño*, is placed in a **cigar mold and press,** which will help the cigar learn its shape. The cigar bunches can be rotated every thirty to forty-five minutes, several times, to avoid creating any seams.

Applying the **wrapper** to the bunch takes a great deal of precision and finesse. First, the leaf (half) being used must be trimmed with the *chaveta* to cover the cigar perfectly.

Torcedores will use every finger, independently, to stretch the wrapper leaf and wrap the bunch. Cigars are rolled both right-to-left and left-to-right, depending on which side of the wrapper leaf is used.

There are a variety of **head finishing** techniques for *parejos* and *figurados*. Each one requires different skills and comes with its own set of pros and cons: see *flag, flag and cap*, and *triple-cap*.

A bit of *goma*, a natural vegetable gum, will be applied to the head of a cigar to ensure that it stays together. On parejos, the **cap** is a round cut out of the leaf that is placed on top of the head to finish the cigar.

After being rolled, cigars will be measured, weighted, and smoked to ensure quality control. Then, they will go to **marrying**, or dehumidification, rooms to stabilize and lose humidity for about a week.

Cigars are moved to aging rooms to begin their **cigar** *añejamiento.* The cigars will be released months or years later when the cigar maker feels they are ready to be banded, boxed, sold, and smoked.

As useful as these pictures may be, there is no way to appreciate the art of cigar making without experiencing it in person or seeing it "live." Furthermore, the *Seed to Cigar* section of this book, while thorough, is a mere snapshot of the world of luxury tobacco . . . a grain of sand representing a desert. Every stage in the cigar making process requires unrivaled levels of human skill, generations of knowledge, artistry, perfection, and sometimes a little luck. Everything from the natural beauty of cigar plants thriving in a tropical valley, the dexterity of cigar rollers, and the special qualities of a wrapper leaf are beyond the ability of words and pictures to communicate. It is practically a miracle that rustic leaves can be grown, processed, bunched, pressed, and wrapped into such beautiful, unique, and delicious objects. Since simple pictures and words cannot do these products justice, we would be remiss if we did not encourage you to visit the TU website to watch the extensive collection of agricultural, processing, cigar rolling, and packaging videos to enhance your appreciation.

CIGAR ANATOMY

Cigar Rolling

The artistry that goes into creating a cigar starts in the fields and culminates in the cigar roller's hands. Whether using **entubado**, **accordion**, or **book** bunching techniques, or finishing the head of a *parejo* or *figurado*, the finesse and skill required to roll a cigar is profound and easily appreciated by anyone. Cigars are far more than a simple bunch of leaves. In fact, most people who have never smoked a cigar still marvel when they have the opportunity to see one made. It is a beautiful art form that must be seen to be fully appreciated.

Today's cigar consists of wrapper, binder, and filler leaves. While there is plenty of evidence of tobacco smoking going back thousands of years and indigenous Americans priming, fermenting, aging, and rolling tobaccos by the time Columbus encountered them, it took until 1676 for the wrapper/binder/filler construction method to evolve in Sevilla, Spain. Since then, little has changed in terms of the construction of premium cigars.

> **TOBACCONIST TIP:**
> Bunching techniques in descending order of complexity are **Entubado, Accordion, Book,** and the machine-assisted **Lieberman.**

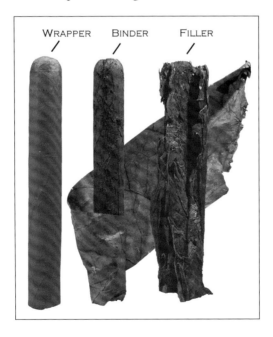

WRAPPER   BINDER   FILLER

The two main types of cigars are **parejos** and **figurados**. *Parejos* have straight and symmetrical sides while *figurados*, or shaped cigars, can vary in dimensions.

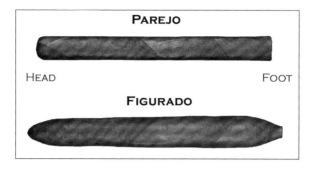

PAREJO

HEAD   FOOT

FIGURADO

Head and Foot

The two main parts of a cigar are the **head** and **foot**. The foot is
the part you light and the head is the end that goes in your mouth.
While cigar heads can be finished many different ways, all of the
techniques require extraordinary skills to create a finished product
that is both attractive and reinforces the construction of the cigar.
The head of a cigar must withstand the extra pressure from your
teeth, saliva, and lips for extended periods of time.

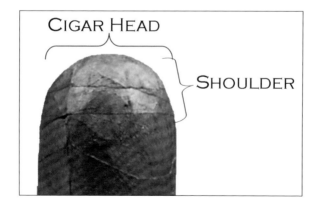

CIGAR HEAD

SHOULDER

Ring Gauge (rg) and Length

Cigars are measured in two ways: length and diameter. In America, the length is measured in inches (") while the diameter, or ring gauge (rg), is measured in 64ths of an inch. A cigar that measures six inches long by one inch in diameter can be written or expressed like this: 6x64, 6"x64, 6"x64rg, or 6x64rg. Sometimes, *figurado* dimensions are expressed with two rg/diameters, like 32/64 or 32/64rg. In these cases, the small rg number reflects the thinnest part of the cigar and the large rg number refers to the thickest part of the cigar.

Figurado Geometry

Figurados with a tapered foot, such as *Perfectos* and *Salomones*, tend to have the most flavor changes as their ring gauge expands. In general, the smaller rg towards the foot pronounces the wrapper and binder flavors more, while the filler flavors begin to express themselves as the cigar is smoked and the rg expands.

Wrapper Geometry

Geometry is helpful when studying the composition of a cigar because it represents the wrapper, binder, and filler proportions. As consumers, we are always interested in the diameter (rg) of a cigar, but we rarely think of the circumference (wrapper + binder) and area (filler) implications. A 32rg cigar has a diameter of 1/2", while the circumference (distance around) of that cigar/circle is 1.57": this means that it takes approximately 1.57" of both wrapper and binder to cover the cigar. The same 32rg cigar has an area of 1963", representing the foot/filler tobaccos. When you double the rg of the cigar, extraordinary changes occur.

A 64rg cigar has a 1" diameter and a circumference of 3.14": the diameter and circumference have simply doubled. More importantly, the area (foot/filler) of the cigar has increased from .1963 (32rg) to .7854 (64rg)—a fourfold increase. This means that when the rg doubled, the filler quadrupled. So, **doubling the rg quadruples the filler**. If the filler proportions stay the same, you can infer that a thinner cigar will express more of the wrapper and binder flavor, making the filler flavors less pronounced.

> **TOBACCONIST TIP:**
> Doubling the ring gauge (rg) of a cigar quadruples the filler tobacco. If the filler proportions remain the same in both cigars, the wrapper flavor will be more pronounced in the thinner cigar. But, cigar makers often change the blend to compensate.

Cigar Wrappers

Wrapper leaves are the most precious component of a cigar. They must be grown, picked, cured, fermented, and handled with extreme care to preserve their flawless appearance. In addition, wrapper leaves must have excellent flavor and aroma qualities because they are said to contribute more than any other leaf in the cigar. While we cannot say exactly how much taste+aroma the wrapper contributes to a cigar, we know it is significant since the flavor will change dramatically if you remove the wrapper from a cigar and smoke it. Try it!

While the color of a wrapper leaf will not indicate the strength of a cigar, it can be indicative of some flavor characteristics. Lighter wrapper colors, like Claro and Colorado Claro, can have a milder flavor. Darker wrappers, like Colorado Maduro and Oscuro, will have a heavier/richer flavor and aroma.

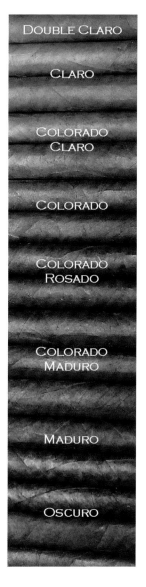

DOUBLE CLARO

CLARO

COLORADO CLARO

COLORADO

COLORADO ROSADO

COLORADO MADURO

MADURO

OSCURO

VITOLAS

Avitola is the name given to a cigar of a specific size and shape. For example, in America, the Robusto vitola is commonly 5x50rg and a Churchill vitola is 7x48rg. Yet, there are no international standards for vitola names, so there will be slight variations from one manufacturer to another.

In America, *figurado* vitolas are even less precise than *parejos*. Vitolas like Perfectos, Torpedos, Belicosos, and Pyramids describe a general shape profile, but these cigars come in varying lengths and ring gauges.

In Cuba, cigar production is centralized and controlled by the state and a joint venture with Habanos S.A. While this system may limit entrepreneurialism, it does allow for more precise vitola standards. Every cigar manufactured in Cuba has two vitola names: first, the *Vitola de Galera*, which is the factory name for a given shape and size. Then, the *Vitola de Salida,* which is the name consumers see on a cigar box for a particular shape and size. For example, a Montecristo A (*Vitola de Salida*) measures 91/4x 47rg and is known as a Gran Corona (*Vitola de Galera*) in the factories.

> **TOBACCONIST TIP:**
> The attractiveness or "look" of a cigar and its packaging/ adornment do not necessarily correlate with the taste+aroma or quality of the cigar.

Today, cigars seem to come in a nearly infinite variety of shapes and sizes, and manufacturers have invented just as many names to describe them. The American market vitolas depicted in this chapter are a good sample of general vitolas, but there will always be slight variations between brands. The most important fact to note is that cigar makers produce specific vitolas to suit customer preferences and convey the unique qualities of their blend. In general, thicker cigars will smoke cooler and longer, while thinner cigars will produce less smoke per toke and emphasize the wrapper's taste+aroma characteristics. In addition, tapered figurado cigar heads can be cut small or large to suit your preferences, and pigtail heads can easily be bitten open.

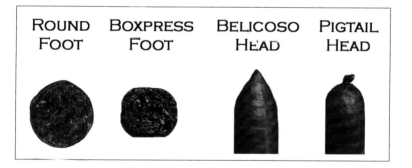

ROUND FOOT   BOXPRESS FOOT   BELICOSO HEAD   PIGTAIL HEAD

TOBACCONIST TIP:
Culebras are three individual cigars braided and tied together. Culebras originated in Cuba as daily rations for cigar rollers. Their under-filled and "crooked" look allowed factory managers to be sure rollers were not smoking the premium products.

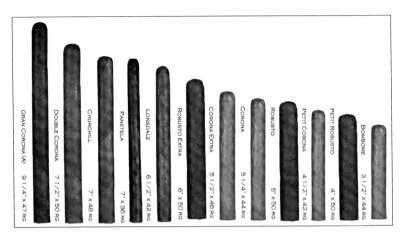

GRAN CORONA (A)   9 1/4" X 47 RG
DOUBLE CORONA   7 1/2" X 50 RG
CHURCHILL   7" X 48 RG
PANETELA   7" X 36 RG
LONSDALE   6 1/2" X 42 RG
ROBUSTO EXTRA   6" X 50 RG
CORONA EXTRA   5 1/2" X 46 RG
CORONA   5 1/4" X 44 RG
ROBUSTO   5" X 50 RG
PETIT CORONA   4 1/2" X 42 RG
PETIT ROBUSTO   4" X 50 RG
BOMBOME   3 1/2" X 44 RG

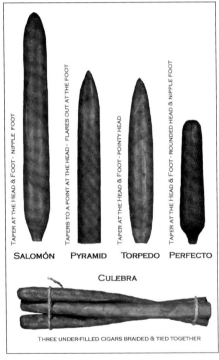

TAPER AT THE HEAD & FOOT - NIPPLE FOOT
SALOMÓN

TAPERS TO A POINT AT THE HEAD - FLARES OUT AT THE FOOT
PYRAMID

TAPER AT THE HEAD & FOOT - POINTY HEAD
TORPEDO

TAPER AT THE HEAD & FOOT - ROUNDED HEAD & NIPPLE FOOT
PERFECTO

CULEBRA

THREE UNDER-FILLED CIGARS BRAIDED & TIED TOGETHER

PIPES & TOBACCOS

Pipe: a device used for smoking, usually consisting of a tube connecting a mouthpiece to a bowl.

For thousands of years, human beings have been using rudimentary tubes, reeds, gourds, shells, bones, nuts, rocks, the earth, and many other instruments to smoke tobacco. There is no way to measure the ways and means humans have used to enjoy their favorite smoke. The only fact is that pipe smoking evolved after the discovery of fire and before the cigar.

Today, great pipe making is an art form carried out by a relatively small group of passionate craftspeople around the world. Pipe consumers are another rare breed of individuals who have a passion for craftsmanship, detail, and the civilized comforts only a well-made pipe can provide. These consumers are very tactile and focused on their preferences. So, any tobacconist catering to pipe smokers will need ample inventory and plenty of time to allow the customer to make their decision.

> **TOBACCONIST TIP:**
> It is common for pipe customers to spend hours in a store feeling, weighing, handling, scrutinizing, and contemplating a pipe purchase. They need time and space to make the right decision.

Pipes—Architecture

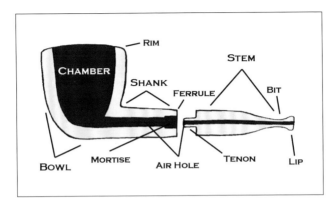

Bowl & Chamber

The **bowl** of any pipe must be capable of resisting hot temperatures and flame over long periods of time. For this reason, the bowl must be carved perfectly. The **chamber** must be consistent in thickness and density to prevent embers from burning through the wall. Ultimately, the value and function of a great pipe begins and ends with the bowl.

The chamber of a briar bowl can be finished in a variety of ways, including *natural, stained,* or *pre-carbonized.* A natural bowl will have no stain or finish applied. A stained bowl will have a color stain applied to give the inside of the bowl an attractive appearance. A pre-carbonized finish mimics the **carbonization** process and leaves a thin coating on the interior wall of the chamber.

Shank

The **shank** of a pipe protrudes directly from the **bowl**, connects to the **stem**, and is typically carved from the same piece of briar or **meerschaum**. Pipes can also be categorized by whether they have a **straight** or **bent** shank and stem. Straight pipes will transmit heat more directly to the palate. Bent pipes can accumulate more moisture at the bottom of the bowl, below the bend of the shank. Great care is taken when carving the shank, since it is part of the bowl and its grain and form must complement the pipe. A well-carved shank will be perfectly aligned with the bowl and stem; it will not curve left or right, unless intended. Additionally, the shank is the weakest part of the pipe because it is thin and has an air hole drilled through it. Shanks come in a variety of shapes and are typically chosen to complement the design of the pipe.

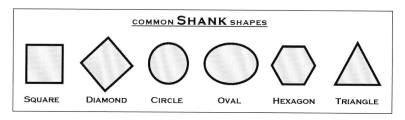

COMMON **SHANK** SHAPES

SQUARE   DIAMOND   CIRCLE   OVAL   HEXAGON   TRIANGLE

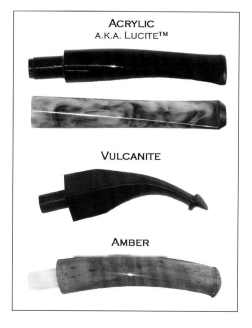

ACRYLIC
A.K.A. LUCITE™

VULCANITE

AMBER

TOBACCONIST TIP:
Carbonization is the process by which char changes to carbon and forms **cake** on the inside of the bowl chamber. This carbonized (cake) material helps protect the bowl from the inside out, keeps the bowl cool, and promotes an even smoking experience.

Stems

The stem of a pipe incorporates the *air hole, lip, bit*, and **tenon**, which typically connects to the pipe at the **shank** through tenon and mortise craftsmanship to ensure a tight and long-lasting fit.

Stems vary in shape and nuance as much as the pipes themselves. Many great pipe makers go to great lengths to ensure that their stems are perfectly crafted to suit the pipes they serve. **Amber**, **Lucite**, and **Vulcanite** are the most common materials for making stems. These materials can be shaped easily and have their respective pros and cons. Amber is natural, beautiful, and expensive. Vulcanite, a type of rubber, has a matte finish, is soft on the teeth, but oxidizes (tarnishes) easily. Lucite, a plastic, is shiny, relatively inexpensive, and can be used to create more colorful stems, but it will still be hard on the teeth and fragile.

> **TOBACCONIST TIP:**
> To clean an oxidized/tarnished Vulcanite stem, you can take it to a tobacconist with a buffing wheel or use a mild abrasive like baking soda to rub out the stain. Regardless of the stem type you have, make sure to always wipe it clean after use.

Pipes: Briar

Briar, or *bruyere* in French, is a dense burl found on the roots of the Heath tree (*Erica arborea*). The burl wood growth is an aberration of the tree's natural characteristics, roots, trunk, branches, and leaves. It has the unique characteristic of being very dense and potentially beautiful when carved and

finished. The Heath tree, which actually looks more like a scraggly bush, is found throughout the dry and hot areas along the Mediterranean coast.

Age

The value and quality of a briar pipe will be affected by its age, since older briar has a denser and tighter grain, which produces very smooth and cool smoking properties.

Grading

Over a century ago, a first-grade briar would have been considered flawless: no *pits*, *grain disruptions*, or *fills*. Today, many first-grade pipes have all of the above. In the absence of international briar pipe grading standards, quality and classifications are determined by individual manufacturers.

TOBACCONIST TIP:
Currently, most high-grade briar pipes are made from thirty-plus-year-old briar. Before 1950, it was common to find briar that was over 250 years old.

STRAIGHT

BIRD'S EYE

TOBACCONIST TIP:
A well-conditioned cigar can age and develop for a lifetime or more.
A well-made pipe can also last for a lifetime or more.

Grain

Since briar comes from a burl, it does not have concentric growth rings like traditional wood. Instead, the wood grows in a randomly tight pattern that is classified as either **straight** or **bird's eye**.

Straight grain looks like stripes while bird's eye (also referred to as **burl grain**) is characterized by tight, circular patterns. The bird's eye/burl grain result at the end of the straight grain, where the wood grows inward and into itself. Both grains come from the same piece of wood and produce similar smoking characteristics. The main difference between the two is aesthetic preferences.

Other sub-categories of grain include flame, random, cross-cut, and cross-grain.

Finish

Generally, there are three distinct methods for finishing a briar pipe: **smooth**, **sandblast**, and **carved**. Briar pipes can also come in any combination of these finishes, be stained in a variety of colors and shades, or be painted.

A smooth finish is sanded and buffed to perfection, while a sandblast finish is achieved by blasting the briar with compressed air and sand (or other small particulates). Sandblast pipes are also called

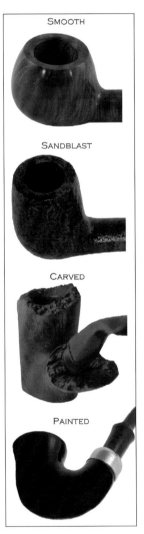

SMOOTH

SANDBLAST

CARVED

PAINTED

rustic or **rusticated**. A carved finish is achieved by shaping the wood texture by hand, with a blade.

> **TOBACCONIST TIP:**
> A professional tobacconist should NOT assume that their taste preference is the same as the customer's. We should ask questions, listen, and try to understand the customer's personal preferences and taste.

Pipes: Calumet

The calumet is a highly decorated pipe made by North American Indians; the calumet has also been known as the "Peace Pipe." Typically, the calumet was made of wood or clay and had a long stem decorated with feathers, animal parts, beads, and other embellishments. It was generally used for spiritual or ceremonial purposes and stuffed with a mix of tobacco, herbs, and other organic matter. While not common today, the calumet has a long and rich history in North America.

> **TOBACCONIST TIP:**
> Over-humidified cigars and pipe tobaccos will produce an acrid and bitter flavor when smoked.

Pipes: Clay

By the early 1600s, the clay pipe was being used throughout Europe. Initially popularized by Sir Walter Raleigh in England, these pipes had characteristically small bowls and long stems. They were sufficiently resistant to heat and could be easily manufactured. The long stem helps keep the smoke cool and gives the user somewhere to hold because the bowl can get very hot.

TOBACCONIST TIP:
A resealable, or ziptop, plastic bag can keep cigars well-preserved for about a week. They are best kept in a drawer at room temperature to avoid air/humidity loss.

Pipes: Corncob

The corncob is the quintessential American pipe. Before large-scale production began in 1868, the corncob pipe was popular among American pioneers and Indians. While the bowl is made from the cob, usually a reed or hollowed out piece of wood is used for the stem and mouthpiece. Typically, corncobs smoke hot and wet and have a limited useful life, unlike briar or meerschaum.

> **TOBACCONIST TIP:**
> The term hygroscopic refers to a substance that will readily absorb and retain humidity. Tobacco, cigars, Spanish Cedar, leather cigar cases, and sponges are all hygroscopic.

Pipes: Hookah

Also known as a *narghile, narghila, nargile, nargila, sheesha,* shi-sha, water-pipe, or hubbly-bubbly.

Technically speaking, a hookah is an indirect smoking system/pipe, since the smoke travels through water before reaching your palate.

The hookah has changed very little since the 1600s. The modern hookah is composed of four (major) parts: bowl, stem, body, and mouthpiece. With the help of water, these components work together to provide a cool, filtered, and smooth smoking experience. As pictured here, hookahs use a hose to attach the mouthpiece to the pipe. A traditional hookah can have one to four hoses/mouthpieces. This multi-hose system facilitates communal/social smoking with multiple participants.

> **TOBACCONIST TIP:**
> Cigar tobacco filler leaves only have half of their
> stem removed, which is the lower, thicker part
> that is attached to the plant stalk.

Credit is given to the Turkish for refining the design of the hookah, as they integrated it thoroughly into their culture and helped spread its popularity. But, long before the Turkish adopted the hookah, it was invented and used by the people of India. Indians and Persians were smoking hashish and opium in their hookahs long before tobacco was introduced to them. By the 1600s, smoking tobacco from a hookah had become common throughout most of Europe. Perhaps, ironically, the hookah is now being used for a purpose for which it was not intended. Consequently, the tobacco had to be uniquely concocted to suit the hookah pipe. Hookah tobacco, also known as *shisha*, is typically moistened with honey or molasses and flavored with fruits and/or spices. The tobacco is kept lit by using hot coals to apply a constant heat.

When smoking a hookah, tobacco is placed in the bowl, and a hot coal is placed on top to facilitate combustion. As you draw air through the mouthpiece, smoke travels through the stem and into the body, where the water is stored. The smoke then filters upward through the water and travels toward your mouth. Drawing the smoke through the hookah is a slow and deep breathing technique because the smoke must travel and filter a long distance and through many parts.

Pipes: Meerschaum

German for "sea foam," meerschaum is a light, white, clay-like mineral that is primarily found in Turkey. Meerschaum has become synonymous with the pipes that are created from it. While it is soft when harvested, it hardens into a porous material that looks similar to ivory.

Meerschaum pipes are famous for their intricate carvings and unique patina that comes with age and proper smoking. New meerschaums are white or cream colored, but they will change to amber and golden brown as they get smoked. Many pipe enthusiasts and tobacconists will only handle meerschaums with a glove to avoid staining it with oils emitted by the human hand.

> **TOBACCONIST TIP:**
> Like other pipes, meerschaums may stay in inventory for a long time. Due to their ability to change color, they should be kept away from smoke and human hands as much as possible.

Pipe Tobaccos

The three main pipe tobacco varietal families are Burley, Oriental, and Virginia. Over time, thousands of popular hybrids have emerged from the original Burley, Oriental, and Virginia varietals, each one furthering its family's genetic development. Some descendants fare better in certain weather or have higher leaf yields, others show extraordinary disease resistance, and still other varietal hybrids exhibit unique taste+aroma characteristics. The diversity, strengths, weaknesses, and ultimate end use of these tobaccos have created a broad and deep family lineage. As with cigar makers, many pipe tobacco makers do not divulge or discuss the specific varietals they grow or use in a blend. Often, they grow varietals or hybrids they developed themselves. Plant genetics are a closely guarded asset for most premium tobacco growers; many consider it their "secret ingredient."

In this section, we will study Burley, Oriental, and Virginia tobaccos at the family level because that is where they are the most distinguished. As you will learn, these tobaccos are grown, harvested, cured, processed, aged, and used differently.

Pipe Tobaccos: Varietal Families
Burley

Burley varietals are light tobaccos that are popular for both cigarettes and pipe tobacco blends. Originally a genetic offspring of a
Virginia varietal, Burley plants are a little smaller than their ances-
tors, but they produce similarly broad leaves. Burley is naturally
air-cured in a process that lasts between four to eight weeks; no
heat or smoke is added. The result is a light reddish to dark brown
leaf with a low sugar content and a mildly rich (nutty or cocoa)
flavor approaching similarity to cigar tobaccos (dark, air-cured).
Burley is the second most popular pipe tobacco in the world, partly
because it burns evenly, stays cool, doesn't bite, and readily absorbs
flavorings and **casing**.

> **TOBACCONIST TIP:**
> Casing is another term for flavorings that can be added to pipe tobaccos,
> primarily aromatic blends. Casing usually involves applying flavored
> liquids, like honey, liqueurs, and extracts.

Oriental

Oriental tobaccos constitute one of the most unique light tobacco varietal families in the world. They are typically **primed, sun-cured, fermented**, and produce small leaves that are low in sugar and nicotine content. Sun-curing will produce a brighter, yellow-like leaf. Oriental tobaccos are mostly grown in southern Europe and the Middle East; they do not need the same rich, loamy soils required for dark, air-cured (cigar) tobaccos. The Oriental plant and its leaves are distinguished by their relatively small size, which produces the fragrant, yet dry, flavor profiles for which they are prized (smaller leaf equals more aroma). Oriental tobaccos are often fermented after being cured in order to develop their flavor and release their impurities and ammonia. Oriental tobaccos are used extensively in **Turkish** and European cigarette blends, but the best leaves/plants are grown for pipe tobaccos.

> **TOBACCONIST TIP:**
> Of all the pipe tobacco varietal families, Oriental tobaccos
> are the most similar to cigars in aromatic qualities.

Virginia

Also known as "Bright Tobacco," Virginia tobacco is another light tobacco named after the American state where it originated. Today, Virginia tobaccos are the most widely grown varietal family in the world. While most of the Virginia grown in the world is used for cigarettes, higher grade varietals and heavier leaves are used for producing pipe tobaccos. Virginia tobaccos are naturally high in sugar content and are typically **flue-cured** after harvest. Large-scale flue-curing is done in an enclosed building with furnace-driven heat piped into the room. The temperature is gradually raised over approximately one week while the leaves and stems dry out. This controlled process fixes the sugar content of the leaves at their naturally high level. Virginia leaves vary in color from bright yellow to orange to mahogany brown. Good Virginia tobacco is naturally light in taste+aroma, sweet, and has medium (to high) nicotine content.

Pipe Tobaccos: Special Types

Cavendish, *Latakia*, and *Perique* are the three "special types" of tobacco. They are not varietals of *N. tabacum*. Instead, they are names that refer to tobacco that has been grown and processed in a distinct way. Cavendish, Latakia, and Perique tobaccos are referred to by their respective names because they are extremely popular in pipe tobacco blends. Within each special type, there are also unique differences that further differentiate these tobaccos. As you will learn, Cavendish can come in many degrees of lightness or darkness, while Virginias come in a multitude of colors including red, black, lemon, and orange, each having their own unique taste+aroma characteristics.

Blending

Pipe tobacco blends are divided into two major categories: **English** and **Aromatic**. English blends, also referred to as Balkan, are composed of Oriental, Virginia, Latakia, and Perique tobaccos. Aromatic blends are composed of Burley and Virginia tobaccos with flavorings (**casings**) added (i.e., Cavendish). Aromatic blends are fragrant and sweetened with sugars and flavorings. Whether a blend is created by a manufacturer or a tobacconist, it must balance the tobacco's taste+aroma qualities with each leaf's density, cut, and burn rate.

Cavendish

Cavendish is not a plant or tobacco varietal; however, it is the name for Virginia and Burley tobaccos that have been put through a specific curing process and storing/cutting method. After their respective curing process (Burley is air-cured, Virginia is flue-cured), Cavendish tobaccos are steamed, usually with sugars or flavoring in the water, in order to infuse the tobacco with moisture and a subtle sweetness. After steaming, the tobacco is stored under pressure (**pressed**) for an additional curing/fermentation period. Pressing can last from a few days to several weeks, and flavorings (**casing**) can be added at any stage throughout the process. The color and flavor of the Cavendish will vary between *natural* and *black*, depending on which flavoring is added and how vigorous the pressing is.

Latakia

Latakia is an Oriental tobacco that is **sun-cured** in the normal way and then **fire-cured**. Small fires are created in an enclosed space with aromatic woods and fragrant herbs used as the fuel. The smoke produced by these fires coats the tobacco and infuses its own flavor. Latakia has a naturally "smokey" quality, but it will vary in taste+aroma depending on its origin (Syria, Cyprus, and Greece) and what wood and herbs are used to fuel the smoke. The length of curing will influence the taste+aroma and strength of the tobacco, but the nicotine and sugar levels will remain relatively low.

Today, Latakia is the key ingredient in **English/Balkan** blends and prized the world over for its uniqueness and character. Latakia is the quintessential **condiment** or spice tobacco: too strong and spicy to be smoked alone, but a unique enhancement that will fortify and distinguish a blend.

Perique

Perique is actually a Burley type of tobacco that is grown and processed in St. James Parish, Louisiana, just outside New Orleans. Perique is **air-cured** like Burley, but for a slightly shorter time. After air-curing, the tobacco is placed in oak barrels and kept under heavy pressure. The pressure releases some water content that did not evaporate during air-curing. In addition, the pressure increases the temperature of the tobacco and facilitates a **fermentation** process. Over at least one year, the leaves are removed, rested, re-piled, and re-fermented numerous times. This vigorous process creates an extremely robust tobacco that has a high nicotine content.

Perique tobacco is very expensive due to the time and care needed to make it. Fortunately, Perique is considered a spice or

condiment tobacco, which is used in small amounts to accent other blends.

Pipe Tobaccos: Special Cuts
Cube
Leaves that are cut and shred into small, uniform, squarish pieces.

Flake
Pipe tobacco leaves that have been pressed into bricks and then sliced into broad, flat flakes.

Plug
Also known as Navy Plug, these leaves are pressed in a tubular shape and sliced off for smoking.

Ribbon
These leaves are cut into long, thin ribbons that are shorter and thicker than shag cut.

Shag
The longest and thinnest method for cutting tobacco leaves. This cut is common for **RYO** cigarette tobaccos and pipes.

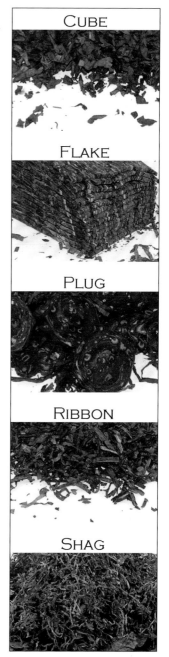

CUBE

FLAKE

PLUG

RIBBON

SHAG

HOW TO

Matches & Spills
Matches

Wooden matches are preferable for cigar and pipe lighting because they will burn longer and broader than cardboard. With any match, it is crucial to let the sulfur (and other chemicals) burn away before taking the flame to the tobacco. Cigar matches have an extra-long shank to assist you when lighting a large ring gauge cigar.

Spills

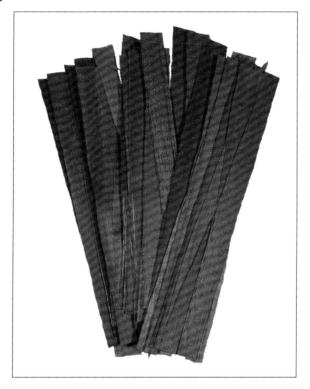

Spills are long, narrow strips of Spanish Cedar that are created from the thin dividers that cigar makers put in boxes. While the aroma and allure of using a spill can add ceremony and panache to a mundane act, they do require another ignition source, like a match.

TOBACCONIST TIP:
The flame of a spill can extinguish quickly while the charred portion can remain red hot. Be careful not to put lit spills in the trash!

Lighter Maintenance
Liquid Fuel

Liquid fuel lighters are functional and reliable. They have the advantage of being simple machines, but impart an unpleasant flavor onto tobaccos. All liquid fuel lighters produce a traditional flame, like the one pictured here.

A traditional liquid fuel lighter contains the liquid fuel inside a sponge, or other absorbent medium, and uses a cloth wick to capture the flame. A simple turn of the flint wheel creates friction and causes a piece of flint to spark and ignite the wick.

Maintenance for liquid fuel lighters involves changing the flint and wick when necessary. To refill a liquid fuel lighter, simply drip the fuel into the sponge reservoir. Do not overfill because excess fuel can ignite. Clean your hands before you attempt to spark the lighter.

> **TOBACCONIST TIP:**
> If excess fuel spills onto your hand and catches on fire, be cool, don't
> scream, and remember that you are a tobacconist. Just stick your
> hands in a bucket of water and pretend like nothing happened.

Butane

Butane lighters are some of the most exciting and functional products for cigar lovers. They have the ability to produce super-hot torch flames, flameless burners, traditional flames, and combinations thereof. In addition, butane has the benefit of being flavorless and odorless.

But, with the use of compressed gas and sophisticated ignition systems (flint, piezo, quartz, battery) comes a litany of potential problems. In fact, professional tobacconists spend a great deal of time helping customers keep their lighters in working order. Luckily, most of the problems customers face are simple to fix, like purging the lighter or cleaning the gas valve.

> **TOBACCONIST TIP:**
> Inexpensive and poorly made butane lighters have been
> known to leak, catch fire, and/or explode. If this happens in
> front of a customer, do not throw the lighter at the customer.
> Simply release the lighter and let it fall to the floor.

Filling A Butane Lighter: Step 1

BUTANE VALVE &
FLAME DIAL

First, turn down the flame dial in the negative (-) direction. The flame dial is usually located on the bottom of the lighter. This precautionary step will keep the flame at a safe level after you fill the lighter.

TOBACCONIST TIP:
Some flame dials can be difficult to access, so having
a small eyeglass screwdriver may be necessary.

Filling A Butane Lighter: Step 2

Second, purge all of the air and butane out of the butane tank by pressing in the butane valve. The butane valve looks and works like a tire valve in that it must be pressed in to release the air. The escaping air will make a hissing sound. Press the butane valve in several times until the hissing sound stops. When this happens, your tank is empty and ready to be filled again.

TOBACCONIST TIP:
Use the back end of a wooden matchstick to press the butane valve. The match is hard enough to do the job and soft enough to not damage the valve.

Filling A Butane Lighter: Step 3

Clean the flame head and/or burner area. This part of the lighter builds up the most char and collects debris. Having a clean flame head is critical to getting ignition and a consistent flame. A swift burst of air from your mouth may be enough to clean the flame head. If you need more power, use a few bursts of compressed air.

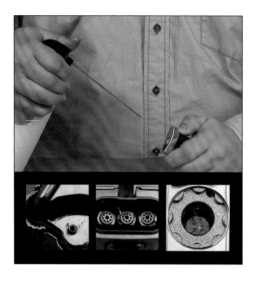

TOBACCONIST TIP:
Burner lighters use a coil to create a windproof heat. These lighters tend to accumulate char since users have to get in close to get a light. Be careful when cleaning burner lighters because the metal coil is delicate.

Filling A Butane Lighter: Step 4

Filling with butane is the final step. First, make sure you use the manufacturer's brand or the most refined butane available, at least triple refined. Quality counts when it comes to butane. Also, make sure the butane you use mates perfectly with your lighter, or use an adapter (commonly included with the butane canister) to get a tight seal. Turn the lighter upside down and mate the butane canister with the butane valve. Press down firmly for ten seconds;

you should hear the butane transfer occur. Repeat this step until the lighter is full, which may be indicated by cold butane splashing back on your hand. Wait a couple of minutes for the butane to warm up, then test the lighter. Adjust the flame to your preferred level.

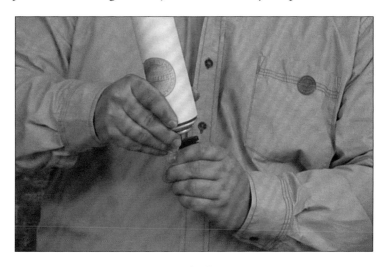

TOBACCONIST TIP:
Butane splashing on your hand feels cold, but it is harmless unless it catches on fire. So, don't smoke while you fill lighters.

Cigar Cutting
The Perfect Cut

The head of a *parejo* cigar has a convex, or curved, shape. The tapered part is called the shoulder. A perfect cut will leave most of the shoulder intact. Getting a good draw on a cigar should require you to remove a small amount of the wrapper to expose the filler. Cutting the entire head off will hurt the integrity of the cigar and potentially lead to unraveling.

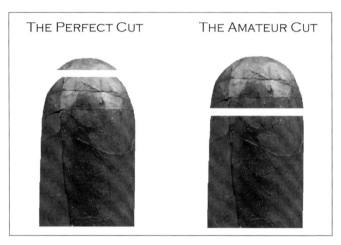

THE PERFECT CUT   THE AMATEUR CUT

TOBACCONIST TIP:
Figurados with tapered heads can be cut to your desired width. Depending on how you look at it, they either have no shoulder or are all shoulder. Customers may appreciate you asking if they want a "small, medium, or large cut."

Whether using a guillotine, scissor, or punch, the first step to making a perfect cut is to get a firm grip around the shoulder of the cigar. Your grip will keep the wrapper from shifting or tearing while helping you guide the cutter blade perpendicular to the cigar.

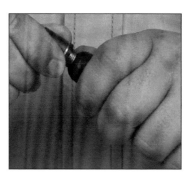

When applying the cutter blade to the cigar, either twist the cigar or cutter to guide the blade through the wrapper; this will inhibit tearing. After you penetrate the wrapper, apply smooth and even pressure to finish cutting through the head. Remember, a perfect cut requires more finesse than strength.

TOBACCONIST TIP:
Tobacco oils and particles can build up on cutters and inhibit their performance. Keep hand sanitizer gel and/or anti-bacterial soap on hand to quickly clean your cutter.

Cigar Lighting
The Perfect Light

Lighting a cigar perfectly requires getting the foot evenly lit without charring the wrapper. Do this by twirling the cigar over the flame to light the outer edges as well as the center of the foot. Many people prefer to toast the foot before they put the cigar to their mouth. Toasting is the process of warming up or pre-lighting the foot. This can be helpful because you can see the fire and get a whiff of the tobacco while the cigar is being lit. While not necessary, toasting can be a pleasing ritual and help ensure an even light.

The simpler alternative is to put the cut cigar in your mouth after cutting, apply fire to the foot, and draw slowly while twirling the cigar around.

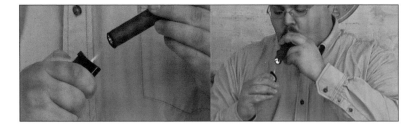

TOBACCONIST TIP:
Whether using a torch, traditional flame, or burner lighter, the visible flame does not need to directly touch the tobacco. In fact, the heat from the flame will combust the tobacco when you draw on the cigar.

Uneven Burn

An uneven burn can result from poor lighting technique, windy conditions, an improperly fermented wrapper, or filler that is bunched too tight.

If the foot of the cigar is burning unevenly, it can be corrected by applying fire to the unlit area while drawing air through the cigar. This should allow the unlit tobacco to catch up.

Touch Up

If a cigar burns unevenly, with one part of the cigar or wrapper burning quicker than the other, it can often be corrected by applying a little fire to the slow burning side. This process is called a "touch up." Touch ups are easy when using a torch lighter because its heat is extreme and precise. When touching up, use minimal doses of fire to avoid charring the wrapper.

TOBACCONIST TIP:
When a cigar is lit or smoking unevenly, it should be corrected as quickly as possible in order to minimize the negative effects. An uneven burn will result in an unintended flavor profile.

Canoeing

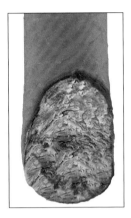

Canoeing is easily recognized by the burning of only one side of the cigar, leaving it looking similar to a hollowed-out canoe.

A common cause of canoeing is improper rolling, which results in tight filler on one side of the cigar and loose filler on the other. Canoeing can also result from improper lighting, wind, or one side of the cigar being overly humidified.

There are two options to fix a canoeing cigar, but neither is ideal. The first remedy is to cut the cigar just behind the problem area and start again. The other option is to burn the wrapper, binder, and filler with a torch on the side that is not lit. This technique will produce a charred and/or unbalanced flavor that will take some time to correct. With a little luck and patience, the burn rate will even out.

> **TOBACCONIST TIP:**
> Even worse than canoeing is tunneling. Tunneling occurs when part of the ember/fire travels through the filler in a cigar and emerges through the wrapper. To remedy, cut and re-light.

Inward Burn

An inward burn is characterized by the filler burning inward as you draw on the cigar, while the wrapper and binder fail to remain lit.

An inward burn can be caused by poor rolling, underfilling, uneven lighting, bad fermentation, and/or short and medium fillers. In addition, an inward burn can be caused by an over-humidified wrapper or uneven humidity within the cigar, meaning the inside filler is drier than the outside wrapper and/or binder.

Fixing an inward burn can be easy, frustrating, or impossible, depending on the severity of the problem. If the problem is severe, it may be best to cut and re-light. Otherwise, you can attempt to re-light the wrapper and filler at the edge of the foot. Unfortunately, this process may char the wrapper and affect the taste of the cigar.

> **TOBACCONIST TIP:**
> An inward burn is what you get if you take a
> match, hold it up to the center of the foot, and just
> take one quick puff. Ever watch people light cigars
> on TV or in the movies like this? Not so good.

Re-Lighting Cigars

It is common for cigars to lose their combustion ("go out") while being smoked. This can happen for many reasons: slow smoking, excessive humidity, or poor bunching/rolling.

As any cigar burns, it transforms tobacco to ash. In the middle of that process exists char, which has an acrid or bitter flavor. When re-lighting, first remove the ash, then gently roll the foot of the cigar between your fingers to loosen and remove the char.

After removing the ash and char, you can re-light the cigar. Take extra care to light the wrapper and filler evenly so they will burn together. Note, after re-lighting, it may take a few minutes for the cigar's taste and burn rate to stabilize.

EXTINGUISHED CIGAR

REMOVE ASH

REMOVE CHAR

RE-LIGHT CIGAR

TOBACCONIST TIP:
Char is the partially scorched, pre-ash remnant of tobacco.
While char may re-light quicker than un-combusted tobacco,
it will taste acrid and bitter, so it is best to be removed.

Tight Draw

A great cigar must have an easy draw. Straining to puff on a cigar will ruin the experience. Additionally, a plugged or tightly rolled cigar will smoke too hot and not allow the flavors and aroma to develop properly.

While rolling technique can determine how loose or tight the draw of a cigar might be, a stem or misplaced leaf can obstruct and completely plug a cigar. The first step to remedy a tight cigar is to massage it with your fingers, find the tight spot, and see if it loosens up. If you feel the plug or obstruction near the foot of the cigar, it may be best to cut the cigar. Lastly, you can use a draw poker or other instrument like a paper clip to gingerly ream the cigar.

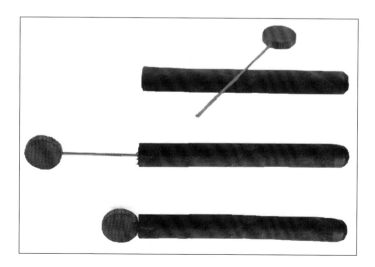

TOBACCONIST TIP:
Olfaction, our sense of smell, is most closely linked with
memory and emotion. This can help explain why people
who hate or love tobacco do so with such passion.

Smoking Too Hot

Great tobaccos have a natural combustion rate at which they must
burn to convey their most unique and special flavors.

If smoked too hot, a cigar will taste acrid and one-dimensional.
Heat will coat the palate, and the intricate blend of aroma and flavor will be lost.

Fortunately, a well-blended and constructed cigar will *tell* you
at what pace it must be smoked. To determine the proper rate of
smoking, let the ash be your guide. A perfectly smoked cigar will
leave a flat foot and ember behind. A cigar that is too hot will leave
a pointy ember behind after the ash has fallen. The pointy ember
is a sign that the cigar is not burning evenly; therefore, it is too hot.
The best remedy is to slow down.

TOBACCONIST TIP:
Premium cigars, due to the use of long filler leaves, can produce a long
ash. A long ash helps control the combustion rate of a cigar.

Cigar Preservation

Cigars are hygroscopic, which means they will release and absorb moisture from the environment until they are in balance, like a sponge. The optimal environment for storing cigars long term is 70 percent relative humidity (rh) and 70°F: 70/70 rule. A well-preserved, or optimally conditioned, cigar is often referred to as "fresh." While this is common vernacular, the term fresh best describes a cigar that was just rolled, not one that is well kept.

Cigars are also sensitive to light and heat. Light can fade wrappers while heat can lead to a tobacco beetle infestation, a tobacconist's and cigar collector's worst nightmare.

> **TOBACCONIST TIP:**
> The 70/70 rule is approximate in that you can or may prefer to keep your cigars within a couple of percentage points of these levels. *Temperature must not exceed 73°F.

Long-Term Aging

Cigar aging, also known as **cigar** *añejamiento*, is the process of organic decomposition under ideal temperature and humidity conditions. Over time, the cellular fabric of cigar leaves breaks down. During this process, taste and aroma changes will occur.

During the first few years of aging, a cigar can become bolder and more flavorful. But, like a bell curve, there will be a climax and then a gradual decline. Conversely, there may be an increase in aroma potency and complexity with the mellowing flavor. Changes in taste+aroma are occurring every few weeks, months, and years. A well-aged cigar will release any impurities like ammonia and acidity, yielding sweetness and subtleties in their place. As the cigar ages, it will give way to nuances, depth, richness, and complexities that were once undiscovered; however, some traits, like strength and spice, may be lost.

While a cigar will age and develop well for a lifetime, the changes are nearly impossible to predict. Fortunately, the joy of long-term aging is discovering the promise of a well-conditioned cigar.

TOBACCONIST TIP:
Cellophane or not? It's up to you. Cellophane does breathe and inhibit moisture loss, so it does have advantages. But, so does letting cigars touch and age together.

Tobacco Beetle

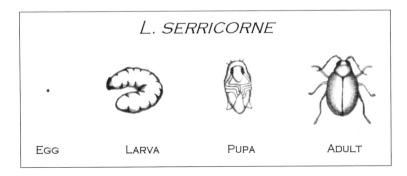

L. SERRICORNE

EGG   LARVA   PUPA   ADULT

Lasioderma serricorne, also known as the tobacco, cigar, and cigarette beetle, are infamous for devastating precious cigars. Microscopic *L. serricorne* eggs exist in tobacco and foods alike. Tobacco beetles can be found in environments exceeding 65°F, and typically hatch in conditions over 73°F, with high humidity.

Of the four growth stages (egg, larva, pupa, adult), the larva stage is the most devastating for cigar collectors and tobacconists. Emerging from the egg, approximately six to ten days after high temperature triggers their birth, the larva live and feed off cigars for roughly five to ten weeks. Larva will eat through cigars, leaving them strewn with holes, looking like Swiss cheese, and surrounded by a fine tobacco dust.

TOBACCONIST TIP:
It is possible to smoke a cigar with beetle damage and not know it. It is also possible to knowingly smoke a cigar with beetle damage and enjoy it.

After devouring your cigars, larva will transition into a pupa (cocoon) and later emerge as adults. While the adult beetle may eat through leaves, cellophane, and cedar sleeves/dividers, it does relatively little damage compared to the voracious larva. By the time you see the reddish-brown, two to three millimeter long adult tobacco beetle, the major damage will already have been done. At this point, it is time to focus on damage control and eradication.

Tobacco Beetle Eradication

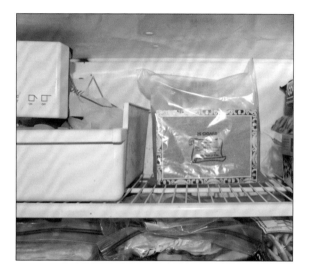

The first step to control a beetle outbreak is to isolate any potentially infested cigars. When in doubt, remove all of them. Pull them
out of your humidor and put them in a box and plastic bag. Clean
out your humidor and remove all small debris like tobacco dust,
larva, dead adult beetles, etc.

Put the boxed and bagged cigars in the freezer for three days.
The box and bag will help contain your humidity. Next, transfer
the cigars to the refrigerator for one day and then return them to
your clean humidor.

Temperatures of 1°F or lower will crack tobacco beetle larva and
kill both eggs and adults.

TOBACCONIST TIP:
Putting the cigars in the refrigerator minimizes temperature shock, but it is probably an unnecessary precautionary step. In fact, you can freeze a cigar overnight, let it thaw for twenty minutes, and smoke it right away. True story. Give it a try. Some cigar makers freeze their own cigars to kill eggs and smoke the cigar right afterward.

Mold

Cigar mold, like any other type of mold, is a fungus that appears as a woolly growth on damp and/or decaying matter, which happens to describe a cigar pretty well. Regardless, moldy cigars are not to be smoked.

Overly humidified cigars are the most susceptible to growing mold. Mold can begin growing before a cigar ever leaves the factory if they are kept too moist or not de-humidified properly. Cigar mold can also result from over-humidification and wet spots in a humidor. Cigars that are kept directly under humidifiers can easily become over saturated. To inhibit cigar mold, regularly rotate your cigars and inspect for mold growth. If you find mold on your cigars, it will not wipe off like plume, so throw them out.

> **TOBACCONIST TIP:**
> Mold can contaminate a humidor. If your humidor looks like it has mold growing on it or in it, it should be cleaned out thoroughly. A little bit of warm water, anti-bacterial soap, and a sponge may get the job done, but allow time for the humidor to dry out before putting cigars back in.

Plume

Plume, also known as bloom, is a naturally occurring by-product of long-term cigar aging. While aging, cigars exude oils through their wrapper. This process produces a lustrous sheen, which is indicative of optimal aging conditions. Over time, these oils dry and crystallize on the outside of the wrapper leaf. The crystallized oil, known as plume, appears as a white powder-like substance.

Unlike mold, plume can be gently wiped off with no negative consequences to the cigar. In fact, many cigar collectors and connoisseurs consider plume a sign of good *añejamiento*/aging. Plume is rarely seen in retail tobacconist humidors since the cigars are constantly turning over/selling.

Humidifiers—Active

Active humidifiers produce humidity through mechanical or electrical
means. The most common varieties have a fan blowing over water

to produce a mist that is absorbed into the air. These units use a
hygrostat, also called a humidistat, to regulate and adjust humidity.

Active humidifiers are common in walk-in humidors and large
cabinets. They are generally hard-plumbed and require electrical
power. Most retail tobacconists use some type of active humidifier
to preserve their cigars.

While active humidifiers vary in scale and sophistication, their
importance to tobacconists is fundamental. In fact, most tobacconists are experts at maintaining and repairing their humidifiers
because they are the critical to the survival of our cigars.

Humidifiers—Passive

Passive humidifiers are intended for smaller humidification needs and have no electrical parts. They work on the principles of evaporation and chemical equilibrium. Passive humidifiers are most commonly seen in desktop, travel, and small cabinet humidors. Note: There is an endless variety of passive humidifiers on the market, and all of them seem to work a little differently. When in doubt, consult your retail tobacconists because they have the experience you need.

Evaporation Humidifiers

An evaporation humidifier simply requires a sponge-like medium to hold water. It is usually contained in a plastic or metal casing with openings for the water to naturally evaporate. The key to evaporation humidifiers working properly is having the proper size unit for the humidor or having an adjustable humidifier that can be manually regulated.

TOBACCONIST TIP:
The first consumer humidifiers, and many modern pipe tobacco humidifiers, are made of hardened clay. The clay brick is soaked in water until it stops emitting air bubbles. It is then wiped down and put back in the humidor. These units have to be perfectly sized to the humidor to be effective.

Two-Way Humidifiers

A two-way humidifier can absorb and emit moisture while seeking equilibrium at a specific humidity level, such as 70 percent. The first two-way humidifiers were referred to as reverse osmosis (ro). They used a generic green foam as the hygroscopic medium and propylene glycol (pg) mixed in a 50/50 ratio with water to achieve 70 percent rh. Today, most two-way humidifiers still use pg to inhibit over-humidification; yet, they can use different hygroscopic mediums, such as crystals or plastics, instead of green foam. Other two-way humidifiers, which do not require pg, can use salt-based solutions to regulate humidity (see Hygrometer Calibration for more info).

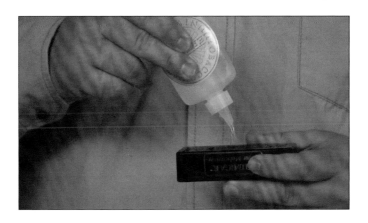

TOBACCONIST TIP:
Humidifiers which use Propylene Glycol (pg), also referred to as a "special solution," may clog from too much pg. Try using a 10 percent pg / 90percent water proportion to start, and add more pg if the unit over humidifies. Or, consult your retail tobacconist.

Hygrometers

A hygrometer is the instrument that measures humidity. The two main types of hygrometers are analog and digital.

Analog

Analog hygrometers react mechanically to the ambient humidity and represent that value on a dial. While they do not require batteries, they do need to be calibrated about every six months.

Digital

Digital hygrometers use electric currents to measure the ambient humidity and require batteries to function. Digital hygrometers tend to be more accurate than analog because of factory calibration and the lack of mechanical wear and tear.

> **TOBACCONIST TIP:**
> The best judge of optimal conditions is touch and feel. Hygrometers can malfunction or be inaccurate, but your hands will never lie to you. Perfectly conditioned cigars should have a little give but bounce back when you release the pressure. They should not make a crackling sound.

Hygrometer Calibration

While methods for calibrating/adjusting hygrometers varies between products, the following techniques will help you establish an accurate benchmark of humidity.

Table Salt Method

Mix ½ cup table salt and ¼ cup water in a vessel, then place the mixture in an airtight container, like a ziplock bag, with the hygrometer. After twenty-four hours at room temperature, the humidity in the bag will be 75 percent rh. Adjust your hygrometer accordingly, or just remember what +/- to factor in.

Damp Towel Method (Less Accurate but Quicker)

Wrap your hygrometer in a damp towel for twenty minutes. Afterwards, the humidity in the towel should be 98 percent.

Analog Calibration

Most analog hygrometers have a movable dial on the back that can be adjusted to reset their accuracy. After using the salt or towel method to benchmark humidity, you can adjust the hygrometer to an accurate position. Use an eyeglass screwdriver, finger, or match to move the dial in the appropriate direction.

TOBACCONIST TIP:
If you want to calibrate your adjustable digital hygrometer, read the instructions. . . . These products are fairly new to the consumer market and calibrating methods will vary.

Humidor Setup and Seasoning

Setting up a new humidor is often referred to as **seasoning** because you are creating the appropriate climate conditions for your cigars. The key ingredient to this process is patience, as you will need to slowly elevate the interior humidity to 70 percent. If you have a Spanish Cedar–lined humidor, this can take several days or a week to achieve, since the cedar must absorb much moisture.

We do NOT recommend wiping the inside of the box with water, a damp towel, or any other type of extreme moisture. Hyper-saturation can cause the wood to expand and damage the joints or seal of your humidor. The best method is to allow the humidifier enough time to do its job.

> **TOBACCONIST TIP:**
> If you want to expedite humidor seasoning, put a bowl of water
> in the humidor to increase the amount of water evaporating
> inside the box. The evaporating water, coupled with your
> humidifier, will speed up the seasoning process.

1. Unpack humidor and inspect for defects.

2. Read enclosed instructions. Note: Many humidors come with inadequate instructions written by inexperienced manufacturers/copywriters.

3. Attach humidifier and hygrometer. If the fasteners (magnets or stickers) are not already attached, you will need to attach them to a dry humidor approximately twenty-four hours before applying humidity.

4. Fill the humidifier with distilled water[1] every day for the first week until you reach the desired humidity level (68 to 72 percent). This will allow the wood to absorb moisture slowly.

5. Once you reach your desired humidity level, the humidor is ready for cigars. The humidifier should be refilled every two to three weeks, or as needed.

> **TOBACCONIST TIP:**
> While many people prefer to have humidors lined with Spanish Cedar,
> a sealed wood can accelerate the accumulation of oils on cigar wrappers.
> Early twentieth century humidors were lined with tin and milk glass,
> which are both non-hygroscopic materials.

---

1   Check humidifier instructions for more specific technique.

Spanish Cedar

Also known as *Cedrela odorata*, Spanish Cedar is neither Spanish nor cedar. Known as *Cedro* in Spanish, this species is part of the mahogany family of trees. Found in Central and South America and the Caribbean, it has also been introduced in parts of Africa and Florida. Spanish Cedar is a hardwood and is naturally resistant to insects due to its volatile oils, which also produce its distinct and prized aromas.

Originally used for cigar boxes because of its resistance to pests, hygroscopic qualities, and natural abundance, Spanish Cedar is the most popular wood associated with cigar preservation and packaging. While the relationship between cigars and Spanish Cedar has existed for hundreds of years, it is not necessary. In fact, due to increasing conservation efforts and rising prices, Spanish Cedar is often substituted with veneers, fiberboard, teak, and other cheaper alternatives. Ultimately, Spanish Cedar is a matter of preference, not a requirement.

TOBACCONIST TIP:
Spanish Cedar is usually kiln dried to minimize the bleeding of sap. If you must remove any sap on your own, a little sanding will usually do the trick. Otherwise, alcohol or acetate may be used, but let the cedar dry out before it is exposed to cigars again.

Pipe Packing

While it may seem simple enough, pipe packing can be a Zen-like art. The technique will have to be adjusted for different pipes, tobaccos, and preferences, but these fundamentals will serve as an excellent starting point.

1. Make sure your tobaccos are an even consistency. Rub out any compressed tobaccos and let the tobacco air out if it is too humid.
2. Fill the bowl loosely with tobacco until it overflows.
3. Compress the tobacco in the bowl about one-third of the way. It should hold its compression but still have a little spring if you press it down.
4. A well-packed bowl will smoke consistently from beginning to end. It should only go out if you let it.

TOBACCONIST TIP:
·When it comes to pipe packing, practice makes perfect. Learn to check the draw before lighting. If it is too tight, you can always start over. If it is too loose, you can always add more tobacco and/or **tamp**.

HUMIDOR ETIQUETTE

Retail walk-in humidors must be rigorously maintained. Their temperature, humidity, air quality, and sanitary standards must be perfectly kept to preserve the cigars and protect the customers that smoke them. People walking in and out of retail walk-in humidors bring germs, dirt, and debris into the environment, so many steps must be followed to protect the cigars. First, tobacconists must regularly dust, sweep, mop, and vacuum their humidors. But, it takes both customers' and tobacconists' efforts to maintain the integrity of the

> **TOBACCONIST TIP:**
> Most dark, air-cured tobacco varietals originated from "Cuban Seeds," so the concept of marketing "Cuban seed cigars" is meaningless. Consumer Beware!

cigars in a walk-in. Ultimately, humidor etiquette is about following the "golden rule" and doing unto others as you would have done unto you. The following etiquette rules apply to both consumers and tobacconists who use a retail walk-in humidor.

No Smoke

The natural aromas of a walk-in humidor are a subtle comingling of different tobaccos from all over the world. Part of the reason tobacconists make their walk-ins accessible to customers is so that they can enjoy the smell of aging tobaccos. Lit tobaccos will overwhelm the natural aroma of a walk-in, and excessive smoke can taint the flavor of the cigars. Not smoking in a walk-in is part courtesy to the next customer and a way to protect the cigars themselves.

Touching Cigars

Ultimately, the head of a cigar will enter your mouth, so cigars must be treated with the same care and respect as food. Maintaining clean hands when touching cigars is imperative. It is important for tobacconists to have sanitary soap and hand sanitizer on hand for personal and customer use. In addition, when inspecting cigars, you should only touch the foot and shaft area. Never touch the cigar above the band (head and shoulders) since someone will eventually put that cigar in their mouth.

Smelling Cigars

As consumers, we all have the right to smell the wrapper and foot of a cigar. In fact, that is part of the enjoyment of picking a great cigar in a walk-in humidor. While smelling cigars can be part of the pre-selection process in a walk-in, it must be done in a sanitary and respectful way, as the nose contains germs and mucus that must be kept off cigars. If the cigar is wrapped in cellophane, push the cigar halfway out of the cellophane. Cellophane smells like cellophane, so there is no point in sniffing it. When finished, you can push the cigar back in. Whether smelling just the wrapper or the foot of the cigar, always keep the cigar at least one inch from your nose and/ or facial hair. One inch is close enough to sample the aroma of the tobacco and far enough away to minimize contamination.

> **TOBACCONIST TIP:**
> The advent of **Lithography** and **Chromolithography** led to the mass production of ornate and artistic cigar bands and labels. By the 1800s, these graphic adornments on cigars helped the cigar industry pioneer brand identity, point-of-purchase, and affective marketing. Cigar bands and labels helped distinguish products that otherwise looked like commodities. In addition, the graphic nature of bands and labels helped market products to a largely illiterate population.

Selecting Cigars

Since we have covered the proper techniques on how to touch and smell cigars, we can address the physical process of picking one out. Some customers take the first cigar out from the top of a box; others like to scrutinize every single cigar. To each his own method . . . there is no right or wrong. But, when pulling cigars out of a box, we must be very careful not to tear the wrapper or damage the head. The cigar foot is highly susceptible to damage. If you take cigars out of a box, lay them in a safe place and return them carefully when you have found your perfect cigar.

Damaged Cigars

One key economic challenge for retail tobacconists with walk-in humidors is minimizing the number of damaged cigars; it is a massive expense unique to our business. While some cigars come damaged from the manufacturers, most damage occurs because of consumer mishandling. Retail tobacconists absorb the cost of damaged cigars since they cannot be sold at standard retail margins. If you see damaged cigars in your retail tobacconist's walk-in, let them know; they will thank you for it. And if you still want that cigar, don't hesitate to make an offer: a 25 percent discount would not be unreasonable for a minor issue.

Returning Cigars

Sometimes, you take a cigar all the way to the cash register and then decide that you don't want it. That's ok. As long as you're handling the cigar properly, you can return it to the walk-in. When returning a cigar to the humidor, it is always best to place it in the proper box with the head up and cigar band facing forward. This is called **facing**, and retail tobacconists do it every day to honor the brand, cigar maker, and our customers. Most retail tobacconists will not allow customers to buy a cigar, take it out of the shop, then return it at a later date. Due to cigars' precise humidification and temperature requirements, plus the fact that they will end up in your mouth, cigars must be treated like perishable food.

Cigar Cutter Etiquette

Cigar cutters touch the head of the cigar that will touch your mouth, so they must be kept clean. Tobacconists must have sanitary procedures in place to keep cutters clean and protect their customers. Every day, customers put a cigar in their mouth and then ask for a cut or cutter. The easiest solution for retail tobacconists is to have two cutter options on hand: a "clean" cutter and a "saliva" cutter. The saliva cutter can be used on tainted cigars and sterilized quickly with hand sanitizer gel afterwards.

Off the Floor

Keeping cigars off the floor is an obvious goal, but it is also important not to place boxes on the floor. Placing cigar boxes on the floor contaminates them with the same dirt, debris,

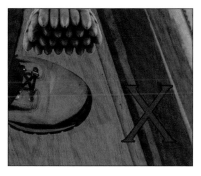

and germs that people's shoes have been tracking in. This piece of humidor etiquette is particularly important for tobacconists to heed because it is easy to forget when stocking and organizing the walk-in.

Slippage

Also known as theft and shoplifting, slippage is one of the greatest threats to retail tobacconists. It is especially common for tobacconists with walk-in humidors. Even small retail tobacconists can lose thousands of dollars per year to shoplifting. The worst part of slippage is that it happens regularly and from the least expected of customers. The video-photo depicted here showed two middle-aged customers stealing over seven hundred dollars in cigars while a tobacconist was in the humidor. Anyone can be a thief, so stay alert!

CIGAR MYTHS

There is enough magic and wonder in the world of cigar making and luxury tobacco to make lies, myths, and marketing exaggerations totally unnecessary. But, that would not seem to be the case since there are innumerable untruths in the marketplace, and many of them have been propagated for decades by successful individuals and companies. Perhaps this is the case because marketers have determined what information consumers receive or because there has never been a credible institution dedicated to teaching, learning, and researching the impressive truths of our industry, but the days of biased romanticism and exaggeration are ending. Tobacconist University is committed to teaching the truth about our industry, not duping customers into brand loyalty and ignorant misconceptions.

Great cigars and luxury tobaccos are practically miracles in their own right. Luxury tobacco takes more collective skills and time to create than many great works of art, architecture, and furniture, but its destiny is to combust and return to dust. Our products need no exaggeration to be fully appreciated; they need honest representation. The following is a list of cigar/tobacco myths that retail tobacconists hear every day.

Virgin Thighs

Myth: In Cuba, cigars are rolled on the thighs of virgins.

Truth: This is an absurd concept that sounds interesting and amusing to some, but it is not grounded in reality.

Cuban Seed

Myth: Cuban seed equals quality.

Truth: Cuban seeds, grown inside or outside Cuba, can produce both good and bad cigars. There is no direct correlation between product quality and Cuban seeds. There are far too many variables impacting the quality of tobacco and cigars like soil, climate, rain, fermentation, blending, rolling, etc. This myth was started after the American embargo on Cuba when cigar makers wanted to enhance the perceived value and quality of their own brands by saying that Cuban seeds were being used. To this day, many uninformed consumers visit retail tobacconists and ask for "Cuban seed" cigars, thinking that they are better.

TOBACCONIST TIP:
The customer is always right, unless you are willing to lose that customer. It's a tough call because every customer is precious.

Maduros Are Stronger

Myth: Maduro wrappers/cigars are stronger.

Truth: While maduros may undergo a longer fermentation, they do not increase in strength or spice. Rather, they become richer and a little sweeter as the sugars develop.

Perfect Consistency

Myth: Perfect consistency exists.

Truth: It is impossible to create a perfectly consistent cigar and blend from one batch to another, much less from one crop/year to another. In addition, it is impossible to construct every cigar perfectly. The nature of handmade cigars requires some deviation. It is okay for a cigar to burn a little crooked and for cigars to taste a little different from batch to batch. In fact, the human senses cannot taste or smell perfectly, so we would not even recognize perfect consistency if it were possible.

> **TOBACCONIST TIP:**
> Perfect consistency is easier to attain in the wine and/or spirits industry, where the final product is a liquid. Liquids are much easier to measure, rate, and blend, so the final product is more likely to be consistent.

Lost and Found [Cuban] Tobaccos

Myth: The classic marketing story about a long lost batch of perfectly conditioned tobacco being discovered and used to create a "once in a lifetime" cigar.

Truth: The "truth" is hard to find in this case. Discovering the how, what, when, and where of a "re-discovered" tobacco is difficult, if not impossible, to prove.

Cuban Cigars Are "The Best"

Myth: "Cubans are the best" is the mother of all cigar myths, probably because it was true decades ago and can occasionally seem true today. Cuba is the birthplace of great tobaccos, seeds, and cigars, but time has moved us forward. Great tobacconists and consumers everywhere know that our *"cigar renaissance"* exists mostly because of the efforts and products created by those outside of Cuba.

Truth: Today, claiming that "I only smoke Cubans" or "Cuban cigars are the best" is merely a personal preference as opposed to objective fact. Aficionados and tobacconists know that taste is subjective.

Spanish Cedar is Necessary

Myth: Humidors and cigar boxes need to be lined with Spanish Cedar.
Truth: Spanish Cedar is not necessary. It was historically and geographically convenient and practical. While it may be a valid taste+aroma preference, it is not required.

Cigar Licking

Myth: A cigar should be thoroughly licked/wet-down before being smoked.

Truth: This practice was common a century ago when humidification was not as accurate and consistent as it is today. Wetting the wrapper would help keep the cigar from unraveling, but it is not necessary when smoking a well-conditioned cigar.

> **TOBACCONIST TIP:**
> Antique humidors from the early and middle twentieth century were typically lined with tin or glass. These non-porous materials allow the oils that emerge from cigar aging to stay on the cigars rather than be absorbed by the hygroscopic Spanish Cedar during fluctuations in humidity.

Angled Cut

Myth: Cutting the cap/head of a cigar on an angle helps aim the smoke directly to the palate and enhances taste.

Truth: In contrast to a *perfect cut*, an angled cut jeopardizes the integrity of the cigar head and may lead to it unraveling. In addition, a mouth filled with smoke will taste the smoke, whether it is aimed at the tongue or not. The other down side of an angled cut is that the heat of the combusted cigar will be aimed directly at the tongue.

Self-Sharpening Cutter

Myth: Some double guillotine cigar cutters are believed to sharpen themselves.

Truth: This is untrue. The physics of metal sharpening have nothing in common with the way double guillotines function.

Packaging Equals Quality

Myth: It is natural to perceive and equate beauty with quality; this is a natural human response.

Truth: Many cigars with simple packaging are extraordinary, and many cigars have extraordinary packaging that is not commensurate with the product. The cigar industry pioneered artistic, intricate, and luxurious packaging concepts, in part, because the products look like commodities without distinguished packaging/branding. But, extraordinary packaging says nothing about the actual quality of a product.

> **TOBACCONIST TIP:**
> A perfect cigar cut honors the craftsmanship and attention that went into creating the cigar. While customers are free to cut cigars any way they like, tobacconists should always provide *a perfect cut*; this will demonstrate skill and professionalism.

Strength Equals Body

Myth: Full-bodied cigars are strong. Strong cigars must be full-bodied.

Truth: A cigar can have a full body, characterized by depth and breadth of flavor (i.e., richness, earthiness), and not be strong. Strength relates to nicotine intensity and can refer to spice levels (i.e. strong spice), but not necessarily profound, rich, or full flavors.

Flavored Cigars Are Made to Attract Children

Myth: If you believe the FDA, flavored and infused cigars are made to attract underage smokers.

Truth: Nothing could be further from the truth. While the FDA claims that flavored and infused cigars are an attempt to lure underage smokers, the cigar industry has no such interest. If this were true then daiquiris, margaritas, and any sweet or fruit flavored liquors and alcoholic beverages could be accused of the same despicable goal. The truth is that adults enjoy a wide range of flavor profiles, including chocolate, vanilla, mint, herbal, etc.

Cigars Attract Beautiful Women

Myth: While sexuality is used by many companies to lure customers to their products, this has nothing to do with the actual product. Many companies that advertise and promote their cigars with attractive and/or scantily clad women are implying that "these cigars attract women like this."

Truth: Using sex and sexuality to sell cigars may get attention or momentarily make the product seem to taste better, but the effect is short lived and hot women are not likely to show up on your doorstep.

Absolutes Exist

Myth: Absolute statements like, "This is the best cigar," "This brand must age ___ months/years," "Dominican tobacco is always mild," etc.

Truth: Everything in the world of luxury tobacco depends on one variable or another. Every batch, type, and crop of tobacco leaf is different. There are no absolute time periods for growing, fermentation, or aging. There are no absolute ways to quantify or qualify taste. There are no absolutes in luxury tobacco, everything depends.

Romanticism plays a big part in the world of luxury tobacco. It is a romantic process to smoke a great cigar, sitting back watching the smoke, smelling the aromas, tasting the notes of flavor, and savoring your time. Luxury tobacco is inherently sensual and romantic. However, real romance and pleasure need no embellishment. The actual magic and wonder of luxury tobacco is enough without the myths and lies. Ultimately, enhanced appreciation requires enlightenment, which requires truth . . . thus, the importance of education.

TOBACCONIST TIP:
The twenty-first century retail tobacconist must focus on products and customers to be successful. But, we are in the business of providing much more than that. In order to compete with the Internet and mail order, tobacconists must provide extraordinary value in terms of ambience, service, community, camaraderie, events, and an oasis from the outside world.

TASTING SCHOOL

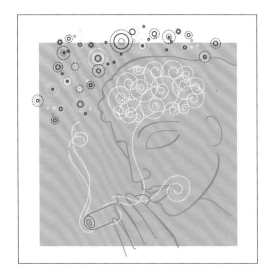

Tasting School, a distillation of Taste College, is an educational foundation for understanding, refining, communicating, and discovering your personal taste for luxury tobacco. It is a combination of science and experience synthesized to enhance both consumers' and tobacconists' appreciation. Tasting School includes valuable knowledge and tools to help consumers and tobacconists communicate their perceptions and preferences with each other. In particular, the words we use and the meanings we intend are paramount when communicating. For example, customers typically ask their tobacconist for a mild and smooth cigar, but they don't always mean that. Even worse, many so-called tobacconists describe practically every cigar in their humidors as "mild and smooth," when they are not. The words we use matter, and the first and most important word that needs definition is at the heart of this chapter and the reason we enjoy tobacco—**TASTE**.

Taste

1) *verb.* The act of perceiving and experiencing the flavor (taste+aroma) of something. 2) **a:** *noun.* The human sense that perceives and distinguishes salty, sweet, sour, bitter, and umami flavors. **b:** An individual preference or inclination.

Taste, as an "individual preference or inclination," is why so many of us love tobacco and why others do not. Personal taste is part of the individual pursuit of happiness, an inalienable right. Taste is how we define and savor our human experience; it is something we are born with and develop. Therefore, no government, legislator, business, or person can take away your natural taste for tobacco. Our taste for tobacco is no less valid than someone's taste for chocolate, exercise, or the color green. The fact that we live in an age that demonizes our taste is a shame. Shame on those who think they have the right to determine our individual preferences and inclinations!

As you read through this chapter, you should feel empowered and comforted by your natural taste for luxury tobacco. It is an enlightened human pleasure enjoyed by civilized people. The only other goal we could hope for is to help enhance your appreciation and pleasure, hence, your quality of life.

The Human Senses
Taste

1) **a:** *noun.* The human sense that perceives and distinguishes salty, sweet, sour, bitter, and umami flavors.

First, we must start with the fundamentals, the five physiological human senses: *sight*, *hearing*, *touch*, *taste*, and *smell*. Each human sense plays a critical role in the way we experience the environment we live in, our lives, and our time. The enjoyment of luxury tobacco is an *organoleptic* delicacy, a sensory delight, just like the enjoyment of fine wine, great food, a beautiful view, your favorite music, or even a hot bath.

The following lessons explain how we apply our senses to facilitate our enjoyment of luxury tobacco. We will quickly learn how the human sense of taste, as processed through the palate, is just a small part of the pleasure we derive.

Sight

Some tobacconists consider sight the "introductory sense," since it is typically the first sense we use when selecting our cigars and pipe tobaccos. Through sight, we can determine the color, size, shape, and exterior consistency of a cigar and its wrapper. Our vision clearly helps us assess the quality and construction of cigars and pipe tobaccos before any other human sense is employed. A true understanding of sight involves knowing its limitations as well: cigars and tobaccos can be beautiful and perfect to the eye and still be void of any other merit.

After the selection of your tobacco, the importance of sight actually increases. Seeing and monitoring the cigar, ash, or pipe is critical to maintaining the proper burn, pace, and ash-free clothing.

Perhaps the most important gift of sight is its effect on our body, mind, and soul. For reasons that date back to the dawn of man, the sight of fire and smoke have a hypnotic and soothing effect on humans. To lovers of luxury tobacco, there is nothing as relaxing as the sight of smoke wafting up into the air, as if your tension and worries are being carried away with it.

Hearing

With regards to cigars and pipe tobaccos, what you don't hear matters most. Aside from the sounds of good conversation, few sounds are associated with cigar and pipe smoking. Even the sound of "freshness" is silent. But, there are a few distinct sounds occasionally heard from tobacco that tell us something important.

A slight "rustling" sound (as if fabric were rubbing together) may be heard when you squeeze a perfectly conditioned cigar. This soft sound is produced by the filler being shifted or moved. It can be heard in cigars that have been sitting and aging motionless for a long time. As long as the wrapper is not producing a "crackling" sound, the cigar should be in excellent condition, and may even benefit from a slight massage to redistribute and awaken the tobacco.

A "cracking" or "crackling" sound is produced when you squeeze a cigar or pipe tobacco that is too dry. Depending on the extent of dryness, both the wrapper and filler of a cigar may make a cracking or crackling sound. Remember, cigars dry from the outside inward so the wrapper will always dry out first. Dry cigars need immediate attention and should not be smoked.

Touch

There is a lot to say about touch. First, it is the physical sensation of feeling. With our hands, we can sense whether a cigar or pipe tobacco is at the proper humidity. We can even use our fingers to determine the silkiness, firmness, construction, and much more of a cigar wrapper.

Touch is not limited to our hands and fingers. There is a broader sense of touch to mention. For example, the way a cigar or pipe feels in the hand is paramount. As tobacconists, we often hear similar questions being asked by customers: "What size should I smoke?"

or "How do I pick a size?" The answer is different for everyone; however, time constraints aside, the same principle applies: pick a size and shape based on what "feels" comfortable in your hand and mouth.

Now, we can delve into the more intangible aspects of touch: feeling.

> **TOBACCONIST TIP:**
> Pre-light mouthfeel is determined by the size of a cigar and its texture, silkiness, graininess, dryness, hardness, smoothness, etc. Post-light mouthfeel will be determined by, and refer to, the taste and texture of the tobacco smoke as well.

Feeling: Spice

The most important and powerful aspect of touch, or feeling, as it relates to tobacco, is spice (also known as *pica* or *picante* in Spanish). The Chinese and other Asian cultures consider spice a component of taste (the human sense), but, in the case of tobacco, spice is not relegated to the tongue. Spice triggers a physical sensation that varies from tingling to stinging on the mouth, back of the throat, palate, and our nasal passages and nose. The intensity and variety of spice will contribute immensely to the flavor (taste+aroma) of cigars and pipe tobaccos. Ultimately, the balance of spice can determine whether a particular tobacco is smokable or not.

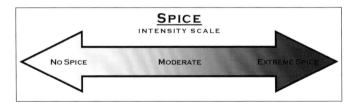

Feeling: Heat

Heat is the sensation we feel in our mouth when a cigar or pipe bowl is nearing its end or burning too hot. If a cigar is *smoking too*

> **TOBACCONIST TIP:**
> Another definition of spice(s) refers to aromatic vegetable products, such as pepper or chilies, used to season and flavor foods. Tobacco spice can take on a variety of flavor (taste+aroma) qualities, just like there are innumerable strength, taste, and aroma qualities attributed to different types of chili peppers. Hence, tobacco can be perceived as having different spices or notes of flavor.

hot or producing unpleasant heat, it may indicate a defect in construction or quality. Heat on the palate can interfere with the way we taste or perceive the flavors of tobacco, so it must be minimized.

In a pipe, premature heat may indicate poor bowl packing or construction issues with the pipe. The heat from a bad quality briar can make the bowl unmanageable or combust the wood itself. Ultimately, pipes and pipe tobaccos are prized for their construction and quality when they deliver a "cool" smoke from beginning to end.

> **TOBACCONIST TIP:**
> In order for people to perceive (sense) a substance through taste or smell, it must be present in sufficient concentrations. Individual sensitivity will vary for everyone, and there is no limit to personal preferences. An **absolute threshold** is the smallest concentration of a substance that can be detected by our senses; like one puff of smoke in a room may be the minimum amount for someone to detect the tobacco aroma. The **terminal threshold** is the extreme point of saturation where the addition of more stimuli will not yield any more sensation—for example, if ten are smoking cigars in a room, the eleventh cigar will not change what you smell. Somewhere between these two extremes lies a pleasurable experience. These **sensory thresholds** are different for everybody. So, a tobacco that is too mild for some can be perfect for another. And, one man's pleasant spice is another man's fire.

Taste: Salt, Sweet, Sour, Bitter, and Umami

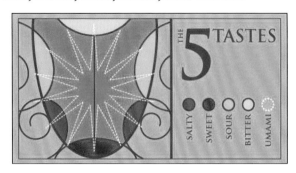

Taste, also known as **gustation**, is the human sense that drives our appetite and protects us from ingesting poisons. We taste with sensory organs that detect chemicals called **taste buds,** which are located on our tongue. Our taste buds will perceive varying levels of intensity, but they are limited to sensing only five distinct tastes: **salt**, **sweet**, **sour**, **bitter**, and **umami**.

It is important to note that we have taste buds spread all over our tongues to differentiate the five tastes, but we perceive these tastes to have a more localized effect. For example, we perceive sourness on the outer sides of our tongue, bitterness on the back, sweetness and saltiness on the tip, and umami throughout.

Salt
Saltiness is the taste produced by sodium chloride (and other salts). As with food, the perfect amount of salt can make flavor come alive, too much can ruin, and too little can make flavor fall flat.

Sweet
Sweetness is typically produced by the presence of sugars in a substance. Sweet flavors in natural (unflavored) tobaccos can be subtle or pronounced.

Sour

Sourness, or tartness, is an indicator of *acidity* or *acids* in a substance. Too much acidity will inhibit the pleasurable flavors of tobacco from emerging.

Bitter

Bitterness is usually an indicator of *alkaloids* or an *alkaline* substance. Bitter taste is characterized as dry and/or astringent; similar to the flavor of black coffee or quinine (tonic water). Among other effects, tobacco fermentation releases ammonia, which is an alkaline compound. Ultimately, extreme or unbalanced bitterness in tobacco will taint the other flavors and finish.

Umami

Umami is often defined as savory, or *sabroso* in Spanish. For many people, umami has a mouthwatering effect and creates a tantalizing sensation all over the tongue (it has also been described as "deliciousness"). The umami taste is common in fermented foods, aged cheeses, meat, ketchup/tomatoes, mushrooms, bouillon/broth, soy sauce, MSG, and breast milk. Specifically, umami is the taste of L-glutamate, the dominant amino acid in living things; it is released through rotting, fermentation, and cooking.

Many cigar makers use the Spanish word *sabroso* to describe the perfect balance of saltiness, bitterness, sourness, and sweetness in tobacco. That synergistic balance creates a sensation that transcends the potential of each individual taste and creates something more extraordinary and complete: umami.

Smell

Smell, also known as **olfaction**, is the human sense contained in the nasal cavity that detects microscopic molecules released by substances like food, smoke, flowers, and wine. Our olfactory nerve cells can detect thousands of distinct scents or aromas that our sense of taste cannot.

Without our sense of smell, it would be difficult for our palate (sense of taste) to distinguish between an orange and coffee or chocolate and vanilla. Ultimately, smell is the sense that reveals the extraordinary qualities of great tobacco, food, wine, and even air. If you don't believe this, try smoking a cigar with cotton stuffed up your nose.

> **TOBACCONIST TIP:**
> If you want to dissect a cigar and understand the individual components and their aromas, you can perform an **aromatic ashtray analysis**. First, take the cigar apart and separate the wrapper, binder, and different filler leaves. The filler leaves will be distinguished by their color and texture. Then, light the individual components in an ashtray, one at a time, and smell the aromas. Keep a bucket of water handy in case the fire/embers get out of hand.

We smell in two distinct ways: retronasally and orthonasally. These can affect the way we perceive a substance.

Thanks to the connection between our mouth and our sinuses, we can sense odors that originate from substances in our mouth, which is called **retronasal olfaction**, and it is particularly critical to the process of eating and gustation. Retronasal olfaction has the benefit of being compounded with the simultaneous use of our sense of taste, so our sensations and perceptions are synergized.

Orthonasal olfaction is the process of smelling odors that travel directly through the nose to the olfactory nerves; this can be focused by wafting the stream of tobacco smoke under your nose. Those smells delivered directly through the nose (orthonasally) can be more pronounced and/or nuanced than those delivered through the mouth (retronasally).

TOBACCONIST TIP:
The act of moving smoke from the back of the mouth, up through the sinuses, and exhaling through the nasal passages is called retro-haling. In order to retro-hale, the mouth and sinuses can be connected by making a "gulping" action and exhaling through the nose at the same time. Retro-haling creates a powerful synergy of taste and smell where the spices, body, flavor, and strength of the cigar will be pronounced simultaneously.

Smell, Memory, and Emotions

The power of an odor to trigger memories and emotions is remarkably strong. In fact, signals from our olfactory region (in our nasal cavity) travel directly through the limbic system, which is the part of our brain responsible for memory and emotions. For this reason, smells/aromas/odors can prompt amazingly vivid memories and trigger extreme emotional responses from people.

Therefore, it is not surprising that lovers of luxury tobacco typically have fond memories of the aromas associated with it. Many people who love cigars or pipes had a loving relative or friend that shared their passion with them. Other aficionados remember the special moments, conversations, experiences, and good times they had while smoking or smelling great tobacco. In fact, the aromas we sense during positive experiences help anchor those emotions deeper into our brains and psyche. So, a great cigar or pipe tobacco can literally improve the quality of your life.

In addition, studies also show that memory retention is improved if a pleasant smell is used while you study and then reintroduced during test taking.[2]

On the other hand, many people who abhor the aroma of tobacco had a negative experience or association with it at a younger age. Or, they believe every negative thing they have heard about smoking, and have anchored their negative emotions.

Contemporary tobacconists can attest to the extreme dislike anti-tobacco zealots can exhibit towards cigar and pipe smokers. People who dislike smoke frequently pick up their pace, cover their nose, fake cough, and give tobacconists the "evil eye" when they walk past our storefronts. In fact, some come in and hurl insults at us. Alas, this extreme emotional reaction is not merely a reaction to the wholesale demonization of all tobacco: **smokerism**. Like Pavlov's dogs, many people who despise smoke are locked into a visceral reaction that has been formed deep within their brain and closed their mind. It is not necessarily their fault that they will never be able to appreciate the delicacy of great tobacco. As aficionados, we must forgive them for their involuntary judgments. In that process, we must also fight any person or institution that inhibits or prohibits us from defining and pursuing our individual happiness. As a minority, this is our greatest challenge.

---

2   Tobacconist University strongly suggests you enjoy a fine cigar or pipe tobacco while studying the academic curriculum. Furthermore, for your academic benefit, smoking is encouraged during test taking.

TOBACCONIST TIP:
The belief of moral superiority over smokers is called **smokerism**. Since the latter part of the twentieth century, smokerism has become a pervasive global social trend characterized by extreme taxation, smoking bans, stigmatization, and prohibitions.

While a particular smell can trigger an emotion or memory, it is also possible that emotions and memories can affect our response to smells. For example, you could smoke a cigar while vacationing on a beach at the epitome of relaxation and think that it was the best cigar you have ever had. Similarly, you could spend an hour with a cigar maker talking about the cigar they made while you smoke it and think it is the best cigar in the world. Weeks later, you could try that same cigar under "real life" conditions and be thoroughly unimpressed. All things being equal, you have experienced a perceptual bias that affected your evaluation of the tobacco; we call this **emotional taste perception**. For this reason, serious tasting and analysis requires a consistent methodology.

At this point, we have just begun to understand the connections between smells, memory, and emotions. It is difficult to put into words the way a certain smell can flood your mind with warm memories or affect your disposition: it can be a very powerful and personal experience. Ultimately, the greatest gift of olfaction is its ability to enhance our lives through stimulus, memory, and positive emotional reinforcement.

TOBACCONIST TIP:
The word TU uses to emphasize the strong connections between human olfaction/smell, memory, and emotions is **smemory**.

TobaccAromatherapy

Aromatherapy is the use of odors to enhance our feeling of well-being. This is not just a kooky idea practiced by hippies and "new-age" people. In fact, thousands of MRI and CAT Scan facilities around the world use vanilla scent to calm patients, showing that aromatherapy is a valid medical and/or therapeutic practice.

The concept of TobaccAromatherapy refers to the beneficial and therapeutic effects derived from luxury tobaccos, products which are cultivated, crafted, and curated until they are combusted for our sensory pleasure.

TU began using the word TobaccAromatherapy in 1998, while the concept of aromatherapy has been an integral part of human existence for many thousands of years. Whether through incense, scented candles, oils, lotions, perfumes, flowers, food, or drink, humans have been stimulating their sense of smell since before history was written.

Pleasant odors can relax and transform our experiences and immediately enhance the quality of our lives. Stimulating our senses for pleasure and health is one of the most natural and enriching ways we can savor our time.

pH Balance and You

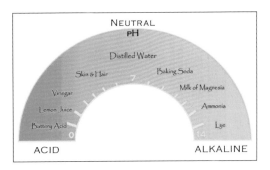

The balance between **acidity** and **alkalinity** affects the food we eat, liquids we consume, our environment, soil, and our bodies. "pH" is a measure of acidity and alkalinity of a solution on a scale of 0–14. Lower numbers are more acidic, seven is neutral, and higher numbers are more alkaline.

With regard to tobacco, pH monitoring is critical for the soil and the water used for irrigation and fermentations. But, the greatest impact from pH can come from our mouths. Our palate's (tongue, mouth, saliva) neutral setting is around 7 on the pH scale. Lemon juice is around 2, tomatoes 4, and milk is around 6.5. Anything we consume will affect the pH level in our mouth, and subsequently, the way we perceive the taste of a cigar or pipe tobacco.

Have you ever smoked a cigar that you know is good and it just tastes "off"? Usually, we just blame the cigar maker, tobacconist, or our humidor, but, maybe it wasn't the cigar. It is very likely that our mouths or senses can be "off." Fortunately, our palates have the ability to restore their neutrality within a short period of time. You can expedite this process by drinking water, sparkling water, milk, or eating plain bread to bring your mouth closer to neutral.

If you just finished smoking a cigar and want another, you can eat a little lemon sorbet to restore some acidity to your palate. Ultimately,

TOBACCONIST TIP:
We use our sense of smell constantly, always checking the air for pollutants, danger, and every other possible stimulus. Our arousal to smell is strongest when we first perceive it. We naturally become desensitized after a few minutes of exposure so we can detect changes in our environment; this process is called **Sensory Adaptation.** This process is exemplified by the strong smell of tobacco we sense when we enter a retail tobacconist and how that diminishes after a few minutes.

maybe you like the contrasting acidity of coffee with the alkalinity of a cigar; if so, great. But, it is good to know the facts and be aware of how our senses can be biased.

Nicotine

Nicotine is a naturally occurring organic compound in the same family of substances (alkaloids) as caffeine. Nicotine is found in tobacco plants and, to a lesser degree, in tomatoes, green peppers, potatoes, and eggplant. The general effects of **nicotine** are **biphasic**: initially it is mentally invigorating, and then it leads to a relaxing effect.

Like alcohol and caffeine, nicotine can be addictive, and its effects will vary depending on the user and delivery method. By design, cigarette smoke is acidic and meant to be inhaled into the lungs where it is easily absorbed in large quantities. Alternately, cigar and pipe tobacco smoke is alkaline and is not meant to be inhaled into the lungs. Therefore, the overwhelming majority of pipe and cigar smokers do not exhibit nicotine addiction because they do not inhale. With regard to cigarettes, it is imperative to understand that the absorptive capacity of the lungs is hundreds of times greater than the tissue in the mouth. Thus, far more nicotine is passed into the bloodstream, at a quicker rate, when smoke is inhaled. The lung-specific delivery method and concentration of nicotine, coupled with the instantaneous effects of inhalation, are what make cigarette smoking a potentially compulsive and/or addictive behavior. This potent, near instantaneous "high" is profoundly different from the experience of cigar and pipe smokers who absorb nicotine through the mouth.

Strength

Traditionally, we do not think of nicotine as something we touch, but it is definitely something we feel. As with caffeine and alcohol, every person has a different tolerance level to nicotine; too much nicotine can induce nausea and light-headedness. Consequently, cigars and pipes should be smoked on a full stomach, when the body is properly fortified.

The effects or quantity of nicotine are what determines the **strength** of a cigar or pipe tobacco. It can be said that a particular tobacco has strong spice or strong flavor, but these are, more accurately, flavor (taste+aroma) descriptions. Ultimately, the true strength of a balanced cigar or pipe tobacco should come from the nicotine, not the flavor.

> **TOBACCONIST TIP:**
> On November 23, 1998, after years of litigation between state courts and the cigarette industry, leading US cigarette manufacturers signed an agreement with the Attorneys General of forty-six states, five US territories, and the District of Columbia, known as the Master Settlement Agreement, or MSA. Previous agreements were already signed with the other four states. Collectively, these agreements are known as the state Tobacco Settlement Agreements, or TSA. These agreements had the effect of making the cigarette industry the most regulated and highly taxed industry in America and has the unique distinction of making this the only industry legally required to fund its own opposition.

Tobacco vs. Cigarettes

There has never been a product that is both loved and hated as much, or by so many people, as the cigarette. There are those who exalt its pleasures while others consider it evil and crusade to eliminate its use and existence.

Today, approximately 95 percent of the money generated by the tobacco industry is from cigarettes. As a result, most people associate the word tobacco with cigarettes. When people discuss the negative health effects of "tobacco," they actually mean "cigarettes." Print publications, the media, politicians, and even the *TSA/MSA* agreements use the word "tobacco" when referring specifically to "cigarettes." In the public realm, there is little distinction made between different types of tobacco, consumers, or consumption patterns. "Tobacco" is a bad word in contemporary society, yet this is misleading. The political, social, and cultural turmoil over one product, cigarettes, has besmirched a much broader and more profound industry.

> **TOBACCONIST TIP:**
> If 10 percent of cigarette smokers in America converted to cigars, it would double the size of the cigar market.

Tasting Methodology

People enjoy luxury tobacco on many different levels and for different reasons. To some, a great cigar can be a meditative or transcendental experience, while to others it can simply be something to puff on while playing a round of golf. Some people taste vanilla, leather, and nutmeg while others just taste tobacco. Ultimately, there is no right or wrong because taste is subjective, and the best cigar or pipe tobacco in the world is your favorite. While there may be more gifted "tasters" or palates in the world, that does not mean that they enjoy their tobacco any more than others.

The TU **Tasting Methodology** is a simple set of guidelines to follow if you are trying to evaluate the qualities of a cigar (or pipe tobacco). This is especially useful for tobacconists who must evaluate cigars for their inventories and then describe them to their customers. Following the Tasting Methodology, or conducting a "tasting," requires focus and purpose because it takes more effort than just enjoying a cigar or pipe tobacco. The three tasting steps are simple enough:

Observation, Description, and Comparison
Evaluation
Pre-Observation: Establish Neutrality

The most important step before tasting is to establish a neutral setting, starting with the pH in your mouth and eliminating distractions. Distractions can include people, stress, other tobacco smoke in the air, food odors, and anything else that detracts from focusing on the tasting. Other confounders include food and beverages, which should be avoided during a tasting since they will change the flavors you are perceiving. In addition, emotional biases can also confound a tasting. As previously mentioned, smoking a cigar on vacation or under particularly pleasant and relaxed circumstances can make the product seem to taste better. Establishing neutrality is about trying to eliminate any potential biases, and this includes physical as well as emotional issues. Finally, if you are tasting on a regular basis, you should try to keep the variables as consistent as possible. This means, tasting at the same time of day and in a consistent place. Again, always minimize distractions and confounders.

TOBACCONIST TIP:
Part of the joy of luxury tobacco is the emotional component, and eliminating so-called distractions can be tedious. In the end, tasting is work. Regardless, neutrality is important, as even the most experienced tobacconists have enjoyed a cigar with a cigar maker, purchased it, then wondered months later why it doesn't sell or taste as good as the first time they tried it. Even professionals can be emotionally biased!

The three steps in our Tasting Methodology are:

Observation

Description & Comparison

Evaluation

Observation is the process of using your senses to observe and experience the cigar.

Pre-Smoke: Appearance, Construction, Draw

As we have already learned, all of our senses are used to savor a cigar, and the process starts before the product is lit. First, we observe appearance and construction with our sight. Then we touch the head and body of the cigar, judging firmness, conditioning, texture, and consistency. Next, we can smell the *bouquet* of both the foot and the cigar wrapper. Last, we can cut the cigar and put it in our mouth to assess the draw and the nuances of the wrapper leaf. By removing the cigar from our palate, we can focus on the finish of the unlit tobacco. The **finish** is the flavor (taste+aroma) that remains after the cigar has left your mouth. All of this "cigar foreplay" will lead to greater enjoyment and appreciation of the cigar you are about to smoke.

Smoking: Combustion, Smoke, Ash, Flavor

Next, we smoke the cigar and assess its combustion, smoke, and ash. The cigar will need to burn evenly for the flavors to develop properly. In addition, a good ash will stay firm until it is released. The smoke of luxury tobaccos will have a distinct texture and appearance as well. While smoking, we focus on the flavors (taste+aroma), strength, spice, body, and the overall experience the tobacco conveys. Every puff of a cigar will yield different flavors. Cigars are blended to change and develop. The unique construction of cigars allows for leaf placements, which will create flavor changes as the cigar is smoked. In fact, cigars can deliver an evolving flavor experience designed by the cigar maker, which is why cigars should be smoked from beginning to end, in one "sitting," the same way you might watch a good movie or eat a great meal. It is also one of the reasons we start smoking by the head and not the foot.

Post-Smoke: The Finish

Lastly, every puff will reveal new flavors and leave a new finish on your palate. The final **finish** of a cigar will be very important because the flavors and sensations will stay with you and evolve even after the cigar is done being smoked.

Description & Comparison

This is the process of ascribing values, measurements, and words to your observations. Your vocabulary, memory, knowledge, and experience will contribute to your ability to describe what you have perceived. Ultimately, describing what you taste is an artistic process because it is an intangible interpretation of experiences and perceptions. Using colorful words and analogies is perfectly acceptable. Regardless of how technical or verbose you are, the only goal that matters when describing a cigar or pipe tobacco is that others understand what you are saying. Unique descriptors like "musty," "earthy," "cocoa," or "nuttiness" are only useful if it makes sense to your audience. The descriptive process is something you can get better at, and there are many publications and experts worth learning from. In addition, having the experience and ability to compare one tobacco product, or cigar, to another is a useful tactic. It can be easier to describe something in contrast to another, rather than coming up with the perfect descriptor. But, there does not have to be a right or wrong way to describe what you have perceived. At this point, the fundamental knowledge contained in Tasting School should be enough to get you started on describing and communicating what you taste.

Evaluation

As consumers, we can usually decide if we like a cigar or pipe tobacco after smoking it. In fact, we probably do not need to go through the rigors of the Tasting Methodology. Just smoking a few cigars or bowls of a tobacco can be enough to know if we "like" something. But, the rationale of tasting is to come to some sort of conclusion—an evaluation.

The Tasting Methodology evaluation should lead to an assessment based on the observation, description, and analysis, but it must also factor in one more variable: the product price. While price may not seem like an obvious part of Tasting Methodology, it is important since we are tasting products, and all products have a price. The ultimate value of a product must be related to its price.

Finally, how we choose to add up all these variables and perceptions is a subjective process, just like taste. You can create a hundred point, five star, or other system that attempts to quantify your analysis and evaluation. The main goal of any evaluation method is for you and your audience to understand it. As we have said, taste is subjective, and how you evaluate and define your taste will be up to you.

Tobacconists, on the other hand, have another burden when tasting cigars and other tobacco products. Tobacconists are buying for thousands of people and investing money that has an expected rate of return. In addition, the cigars we taste must fit into our inventory and provide some compelling value. They must be distinctive in order to compete and satisfy consumers. In the end, tobacconist tasting evaluations will define our businesses and impact our customers. Consequently, our evaluations will play a large role in determining how our customers evaluate us.

> **TOBACCONIST TIP:**
> Due to the unique, handmade nature of cigars and their natural leaf composition, a fair tasting should include more than one cigar. In fact, your knowledge and appreciation of a particular cigar will grow with each one you smoke. Customers should be aware that tasting a cigar just once is probably not enough to make an educated decision. Smoke a box!

Cigar Pairing

There is a perfect cigar for every activity and occasion. As tobacconists, we need to understand our customers' preferences to make the best recommendations. This means we must ask the right questions. People smoke cigars for different reasons. Some people like to smoke alone, meditate, and relax while doing nothing, while others prefer to socialize, talk, and do things while smoking cigars.

Active cigar smokers may do yard work, play golf, fish, or drive while they smoke. As a general rule of thumb, thicker ring gauge (rg) cigars may work better in these conditions. Thinner cigars may not hold up as well in windy or active conditions. Golfers tend to prefer longer and thicker cigars to hold up to the environment and the length of time it takes to play the game, while someone doing yard work may prefer a shorter cigar. Ask your customer questions to help guide them to the right cigars. Special occasions like weddings, birthdays, BBQs, tailgating, and graduations are great opportunities where cigars are used to celebrate and punctuate special events.

The Weather

Weather is yet another factor which will influence cigar consumption. Shorter and more flavorful cigars may be better for cold weather because fuller flavor translates better in colder air—cold air can desensitize the palate and olfactory senses. Shorter sizes also make better sense for people who have to smoke outside in cold weather.

The Dog Walker

Dog Walker is a relatively new term to describe smaller/shorter cigars which are ideal for the short amount of time it takes to walk a dog.

Cigars For Friends

Cigars make great gifts and friends love receiving cigars! Most people smoke socially and to celebrate special occasions, but cigars also act as a punctuation that can make any occasion special. Many tobacconists recommend smoking the same cigars as your friends because it helps to talk about what you are tasting, share notes, and learn in the process. Smoking cigars with friends can be enriching and educational.

Women Cigar Smokers

Do not assume women want smaller and daintier cigars. Male and female palates and taste are not different. Although women make up a much smaller percentage of cigar smokers, it is important not to assume they want more "feminine" products. As with men, when servicing women, it is appropriate to ask what vitola (length and ring gauge) they will find comfortable in their hands and mouth, but it is inappropriate to assume anything about their flavor preferences.

Weddings

Weddings are a tremendous opportunity to sell and consume cigars. They are also an excellent opportunity to promote the retail tobacconist's business with branded matches, cigar cutters, bags, and nicely packaged products. It is always nicer to package cigars in leftover cigar boxes with matches than to throw a messy bag of cigars on a table. When buying or selling cigars for a wedding, unless otherwise instructed, it is best to play it safe with milder cigars.

Food & Beverage

Pairing food, beverages, and cigars is the ultimate opportunity to enhance your customer's experience and promote loyalty to your business. The right pairings make everything taste better!

Cigars pair well with coffee, tea, beers, scotch, bourbon, rye, port, brandy, wine, and many clear spirits. In general, sour cocktails pair less well with cigars, but if that is your customer's preference, then who are we to disagree? As we learned in Taste College, taste is subjective!

The simplest approach to pairing cigars with beverages and food is to match the body of the cigar with the body of the food and beverage.

Light bodied and milder strength cigars will pair well with less acidic white wines, younger reds, creamy liquors, and pilsner and lager beers.

Medium bodied cigars pair well with Lowland, Speyside, Irish and blended whiskies (less peaty), many rums, bourbons, ryes, ports, some fuller bodied red wines, and some ales, lagers, and IPA beers.

Fuller bodied and spicier cigars may need fuller bodied beverages to hold up on the palate. A cigar that is too flavorful will mask the beverage, or vice versa. These cigars pair well with peaty Islay and heavier scotches, spiced rums, and stouts, porters, and bock beers.

CAUTIONARY NOTE:
Cigar wrapper color/shades do not necessarily tell the story of how flavorful or spicy a cigar may be. While generally lighter colored wrappers may reflect a lighter flavored cigar, this is not always the case. And some darker wrapper cigars can also be deceptive and actually be mild in flavor. Maduro cigars that have been fermented longer to be darker and sweeter will pair well with sweeter beverages and foods.

Flavor Pairing Theory

If you taste hints of chocolate, nuts, spices, wood, leather, or vegetal traits in a food or beverage then those same perceptions can be picked up from a cigar. Pairing similar food and beverage flavors together with cigars is the traditional way to pair well. We call this process of pairing like things together **Like Pairing**. Conversely, you can pair dissimilar things together that interplay, contrast, and enhance each other: think of peanut butter and chocolate, or grilled cheese and tomato soup. We call this **Contrast Pairing**. Both methods are valid, a little subjective, and a great way to experiment and enhance your appreciation of the organoleptic delicacies you are tasting.

Certified Cigar Reviews

After decades in development, TU launched the Certified Cigar Reviews (CCR) website in 2020: it is the world's first and only inter-active platform for creating cigar reviews. The CCR gives profes-sionals and consumers a platform and methodology to document and evaluate cigars. Certified Cigar Reviews are organized by Cigar Specs, Component Data, Pre-Smoke, Smoke, and Post-Smoke. Reviewers rate the objective and subjective criteria of a cigar: includ-ing aesthetics, construction, flavor (taste+aroma), spice, strength, body, and smoking conditions. Facts, sensations, impressions, and opinions are documented, aggregated, evaluated, processed and displayed on a graphically rich webpage, which can also be shared, printed, and/or saved by anyone in the world. Furthermore, all of the review data and criteria are hyperlinked with the TU academic curriculum to enhance the educational experience and establish fundamental definitions and facts. So if you don't know what "strength," "spice," or "body" means, you just click on the word and learn.

The CCR homepage displays snapshots of reviews done by Certified Retail Tobacconists (CRT); just click on the image to see the full review. In addition, CCR users can search for cigars by an almost infinite array of variables including brands, country of origin, wrapper, size, date of creation (DOC), CRT Reviewer, flavor descriptors, pairing recommendations, strength, spice, body, etc.

Certified Cigar Reviews aggregates reviews from the most knowledgeable people in the world and harnesses the data to help educate and inform everyone. In addition, every cigar review can be shared, linked, and promoted through all of your social media and Internet channels as well as printed in the form of shelf talkers and spec sheets. The shelf talkers are a tool for tobacconists to use in their stores, while the spec sheets are a great way for professionals and consumers to print, organize, and bind hard copies of their reviews for easy reference.

While our CCR homepage displays CRT reviews, the website and its functionality is open to everyone. If you use it, you can create your own homepage filled with reviews and visit your friends' pages to see their reviews. We encourage you to take a look and use these resources to expand and enhance your enjoyment of luxury tobacco products. And just in case you don't have access to the web, below you will find a useful outline of the Certified Cigar Reviews framework and methodology.

Cigar Specs

- Brand, Line/Sub-Brand, Line Extension, Special Edition or Nickname
- Country of Origin, Factory Name
- Parejo or Figurado
- Vitola Name, Length, Ring Gauge
- Wrapper Color
- Date of Creation (DOC), Date Purchased, Date Smoked/ Reviewed
- MSRP or Price Paid
- Bundle or Box, Box/Bundle Count
- Number Smoked

Component Data

- Wrapper Country
- Wrapper Region
- Wrapper Seed Varietal
- Wrapper Priming/Special Notes
- (Add second wrapper data if Barber Pole or Candy Cane Cigar)
- Binder Country
- Binder Region
- Binder Seed Varietal
- Binder Priming/Special Notes
- (Add second binder data if it applies)
- Filler #1 Country
- Filler #1 Region
- Filler #1 Seed Varietal

- Filler #1 Priming/Special Notes
- (Add additional fillers and data as needed)

Pre-Smoke

- Smoking Conditions: while driving, dog walking, celebrating/vacationing, indoors-alone, outdoors-w/ others, neutral, outside cold, bad mood, etc.
- Construction: Round or Box Pressed, Head Type (traditional round, flat/box press, pigtail, belicoso, etc.), Foot Type (traditional flat, tapered, flared, shaggy, etc.).
- Appearance: while beauty is in the eye of the beholder, inconsistent color, thick veins, sloppy construction, wrapper patches, uneven shap/bumpiness, color, and oiliness can affect the attractiveness of the cigar: Rate between 0 (Unimpressive) to 10 (Great).
- Band and Dress Attractiveness: rate how you fell about the cigar band(s), ribbons, Spanish Cedar sleeve, tube, and/or any other brand dress that was on the cigar. Rate between 0 (Unimpressive) to 10 (Great).
- Flavor: the pre-light aroma and taste of a cigar is very subtle and different than what you will experience when you light up. Smell the wrapper and foot of the cigar and taste the wrapper when you test the draw. Consider this cigar foreplay, a pre-light ritual to familiarize yourself with the cigar you are about to smoke. Rate between 0 (Unimpressive) to 10 (Great).
- Cutter Used: guillotine, punch, piercer, V, teeth, etc.
- Draw: a cigar that won't draw won't smoke, so this is the most important construction criteria. Draw preferences are

also subjective and vary by consumer and manufacturer. Rate between 0 (Tight) to 10 (Perfect).

Smoke

You can choose to evaluate the cigar as a whole, first/second half, or beginning/middle/end. It's up to you, but the following criteria and methods will apply.

- **Taste**: give your overall impression of the cigar's taste profile—salty, sweet, sour, bitter, and umami perceptions. Rate between 0 (Unimpressive) to 10 (Great).
- **Aroma**: give your overall impression of the cigar's aroma. Rate between 0 (Unimpressive) to 10 (Great).
- **Flavor and Sensation Descriptors**
  - » Flavor is the combination of taste and aroma, use this section to articulate the nuances that you perceive. Some examples of flavor descriptors: bitter chocolate, brown sugar, butterscotch, coffee, vanilla, BBQ, leather, barnyard, mulch, vegetal, mushroom, ammonia, iron, soap, almond, caramel, espresso, tea, cedar, hickory, pine, etc.
  - » Sensations are physiological responses that you feel. Some examples of sensations: hot, bitter, buttery, creamy, salivating, sour, sweet, salty, umami, etc.
- **Complexity**: rate the complexity/sophistication of the cigar's taste and aroma between 0 (None) to 10 (Extreme).
- **Spice**: the physical sensation that varies from tingling to stinging in the mouth, back of the throat, palate, throughout our nasal passages and nose. Rate between 0 (None) to 10 (Extreme).
- **Strength**: rate the intensity of the nicotine in the cigar between 0 (None) to 10 (Extreme).

- **Body**: the breadth and depth (spectrum) of flavor of a tobacco; also referred to as richness and fullness. The body of the cigar's flavor can be sensed as "mouthfeel": a full-bodied cigar will coat the palate more profoundly than a thin or light-bodied cigar. Rate between 0 (Light) to 10 (Full).
- **Finish**: describes the intensity and duration of lingering flavors and sensations left behind by the smoke on your palate. Rate between 0 (None/Light) to 10 (Long/Full).

Post-Smoke

- Smoking Time
- Smoking Issues: list any issues you may have had, including canoeing, inward burn, tunneling, smoked too hot, tight draw, wrapper needed touch ups, etc.
- Overall Rating: rate between 0 (Unimpressive) to 10 (Great).
- Pairing Recommendations: Beverage: note any comments or suggestions you may have.
- Pairing Recommendations: Food: note any comments or suggestions you may have.

Final Thoughts: write down anything else you may want to remember or share.

We strongly suggest you visit certifiedcigarreviews.com to get the full interactive experience of this review methodology and platform. You will get to see comprehensive reviews from the industry's greatest professionals, Certified Retail Tobacconists. And if you're dedicated and passionate enough, we welcome you to use the same system to create your own reviews.

AFTERWORD

It is fitting to wrap up *The Tobacconist Handbook* right after the Tasting School, since tobacconists will be evaluated by their product evaluations. But, as you have read, there are many skill sets and a great deal of knowledge involved in being a great tobacconist. In this "golden age of cigar making," tobacconists must keep up with the world's most educated consumers. This is no easy task! It is our duty to have expert knowledge in every area of luxury tobacco and the products that serve us. We must be able to address and/or fix every problem our customers have, enhance their appreciation, and provide a sanctuary for them to enjoy our passion.

There is an old tobacconist adage that says, "The best tobacconists have forgotten more than I will ever know." And these words ring true to any tobacconist worth their salt, since we learn so much every day, whether from cigar makers, new products, or customers. Some great tobacconists are pipe specialists, super-tasters, or master communicators. But, I have never met a tobacconist that can be all things to all people; after all, we are only human. The best we can do is know our fundamentals, as articulated in this handbook, and strive to learn and teach every day. In the end, if your retail tobacconist can keep you satisfied, enticed, and enhance your appreciation, then count yourself lucky to have an excellent professional serving your needs. It is our privilege to do so.

GLOSSARY

8-9-8: a standard cigar box designed to hold eight cigars on top, nine in the middle, and eight on the bottom. In most cases, 8-9-8 boxes are also **cello boxes**.

absolute threshold: the **sensory threshold** where the smallest concentration of a substance can be detected by our senses; like one puff of smoke in a room may be the minimum amount for someone to **smell**.

accordion (bunch) rolling: a bunching technique in which the outer sides of the filler leaves are folded inward, one at a time. The bunched leaves are then placed on top of each other until the bunch is complete and wrapped with a binder leaf to be placed in a cigar mold. This technique allows more air passage through the cigar than a **booked** or **Lieberman** rolled cigar; therefore, it takes more skill and time to execute. Also called "*arrugado*," a Spanish term meaning "wrinkled," accordion rolling is not as sophisticated as *entubado* rolling.

acidic: having the properties of an acid, or having a pH of less than 7. Acidic flavor is sour and pungent. Because cigarette tobaccos are acidic, they can be inhaled easily, unlike cigar and pipe tobaccos (which are **alkaline**).

active humidifier: a machine designed to create humidity. Active humidifiers generally have a fan blowing on or over water to produce a mist that is absorbed by the surrounding air. Active humidifiers are common in **walk-in** humidors and large cabinets.

affective marketing: the process of promoting a product or service in a way that appeals to or influences feeling and emotion in the target audience.

African block meerschaum: from Tanzania, Africa, this type of meerschaum differs from the Turkish variety in that it is fired at high temperatures, then stained in shades of brown, black, and yellow.

air-curing: the process used for cigar tobaccos (dark air-cured) and for **Burley** tobaccos (light air-cured). After being harvested, cigar leaves are hung in pairs in curing barns, *Casas de Tabaco*, for approximately fifty days. During this process, the tobacco leaves lose their chlorophyll and 85 percent of their humidity.

alkaline: having the properties of an alkali (base), or having a pH greater than 7. Alkaline flavor is bitter, dry and astringent. Cigar and pipe tobaccos are highly alkaline because they have high ammonia content and should not be inhaled.

alkaloid: any in a class of naturally occurring organic bases containing nitrogen. Alkaloids include nicotine, morphine, ephedrine, and quinine, among thousands of others. They are of interest mostly because of their physiological effects on humans and animals.

amarillo: a Spanish word for "yellow," here referring to a color classification of shade-grown wrapper leaf.

amatista **jar**: a hermetically sealed jar containing fifty (or occasionally twenty-five) cigars.

amber: fossilized tree sap, sometimes used to make **pipe stems** for meerschaum or high end briar pipes. Amber stems are beautiful, yet fragile, and may feel like glass on the teeth.

American blend (cigarette): a mixture of Virginia, Burley, and Oriental tobaccos. The amount of each type of tobacco in the blend varies by brand, but generally consists of 50 percent Virginia, 37 percent air-cured Burley, and 13 percent Oriental. The tobaccos for this blend are typically **cased** during the curing process.

American Market Selection (AMS): refers to *claro* and **double claro** colored cigars which were popular during the middle of the twentieth century in the United States of America.

ammonia: an **alkaline** compound that exists naturally in the tobacco leaf. Much of the ammonia is expelled as a gas during the **fermentation** process.

añejador: the professional in charge of *añejamiento*. The *añejador* curates the temperature, humidity, and aging standards for tobaccos and cigars.

añejamiento: the aging process (i.e., the slow, natural decomposition that occurs at lower humidity and temperature levels than **fermentation**). During *añejamiento*, tobaccos slowly develop and release impurities and ammonia. Tobacco *añejamiento* pertains to leaves and occurs after fermentation, often going on for years. Cigar *añejamiento* occurs after the cigars are rolled, while they are curated by a tobacconist, then in a personal humidor until the cigars are smoked.

anilladora: the Spanish term for the worker who applies the band to the cigar.

anillo: Spanish for "ring"; here, it refers to cigar bands.

anniversary: In the world of luxury tobacco, cigars, pipes, and tobaccos called "Anniversary" commemorate a date or event. It does not mean that the tobaccos or products are **vintage** or inherently special for any other reason.

apple (pipe): a pipe with a round shaped bowl reminiscent of an apple.

apprenticeship: a period of service and learning an art or trade.

aroma: a distinctive and pleasant smell.

Aromatic (Ashtray) Analysis: a term used by TU to describe the process of dissecting a cigar to smell the aromas of the individual leaf components. First, take the cigar apart gently and separate the wrapper, binder, and different filler leaves. The filler leaves will be distinguished by their color and texture. Then, light the individual components in an ashtray one at a time and smell the aromas. Keep a bucket of water handy in case the fire/embers get out of hand.

Aromatic blend (pipe tobacco): blended Virginia and Burley tobaccos that have flavorings or **casing** added as part of the manufacturing/blending process. Some common casings are chocolate, vanilla, cherry, and rum. Aromatics are typically mild and have a sweeter taste+aroma.

artisan: a skilled worker who practices a trade or handicraft, often using traditional methods.

arrugado **(bunch) rolling**: Spanish term for **accordion** rolling.

B & M: short hand for a "Brick and Mortar" retail tobacconist.

Balkan blend: see **English blend** pipe tobacco.

band (cigar): synonym for cigar ring, traditionally located below the shoulder; a band may also be applied around the foot of the cigar. See *anillo*.

barber poll: A term describing a cigar wrapped with two overlapping and color contrasting wrappers: looks like a barber pole or candy cane.

barrel: 1) see **body**; 2) wooden vessels used to age tobacco leaves.

belicoso: traditionally, this cigar shape (**vitola**) was a small pyramid between five to five and one-half inches long. Today, the size can refer to a pointed/tapered and pointed head.

bent pipe: characterized by a curved shank and stem. Bent pipes tend to collect moisture at the bottom of the **bowl**, below the bend of the **shank**, but they can transmit less heat to the **palate** than **straight pipes**.

betun: a concoction of water and tobacco residues used to wet down the tobacco before fermentation.

billiard (pipe): a pipe shape with a slightly rounded bowl and straight stem.

binder: dense, strong leaves that are applied to the outside of the filler tobaccos. The binder protects and holds the filler tobaccos together in cigar **molds** and presses.

biphasic: having two distinct, and often seemingly contradictory, effects; in the case of nicotine, the effects of both mental alertness and physical relaxation.

bird's eye: see **burl grain**.

bit: the part of the stem that the lips and teeth rest upon.

Black Cavendish: a pipe tobacco that is steamed, usually with sugars or flavoring in the water, and pressed for an additional aging period. Black Cavendish goes through more vigorous pressing than Natural Cavendish, yielding a darker color and richer flavor.

blend: The combination of different types of tobacco used to create a specific character and taste. In a cigar, this includes **filler, binder,** and **wrapper** leaves from different parts of the plant, different plants, and different regions. For pipe tobaccos, see **Aromatic** and **English** blend definitions.

bloom: synonym for **plume**.

blue mold: *Peronospara tabacina,* an airborne fungus that can ravage a tobacco field or even an entire plantation in a matter of days. Blue mold flourishes in cool, cloudy, humid weather. The effects are distinguished by small, round blemishes on the tobacco leaves.

body: 1) the middle part of the cigar, also called the **barrel**; 2) the breadth and depth (spectrum) of flavor of a tobacco. Body is also commonly referred to as richness or fullness and is perceived as **mouthfeel**. Body should not to be confused with the tobacco's strength or spice.

Bofeton: a flap of delicate paper used to cover cigars in a box, lying under the lid and over the cigars.

boite nature: the classic cedar box in which cigars are packaged.

Bonsack Machine: invented by James Albert Bonsack and patented in 1880, the first commercial cigarette injecting machine, which ushered in the age of mass-produced cigarettes.

book (bunch) rolling: a bunching technique which involves laying filler leaves flatly on top of one another and then folding them up like a book to complete the bunch. This technique is simpler than both *entubado* and **accordion** rolling but creates a less aerated cigar structure. Book rolling is quicker and more efficient from a manufacturing perspective and is probably the most popular technique employed today.

boquilla: a Spanish term referring to the cigar's **foot**.

B.O.T.L.: an acronym, "Brothers of the Leaf."

bouquet: the smell or "nose" of a cigar or pipe tobacco.

boutique: 1) of a manufacturer, a smaller cigar, pipe, and tobacco company with limited production. In general, boutique companies are more artisan-oriented. 2) in retail, a small store specializing in premium and super-premium products.

bowl (pipe): the hollowed out part of a pipe that holds tobacco.

Box press: technique which squares off the sides of a traditional "cylinder" shaped cigar. The traditional Cuban Box Press is a by-product of the tight box helping to shape very humid cigars into a square.

briar: from the French *bruyere*, briar is the name for wood that comes from burls found on roots of the Heath tree (*Erica arborea*). Briar is the most widely used material for pipe making.

bright tobacco: denotes the lighter Virginia tobacco varietals.

Broadleaf: a dark tobacco varietal family popular for producing wrapper leaves that are enormous, resilient, and thick. These leaves are ideal for creating a **maduro** colored wrapper. Traditionally,

Broadleaf wrapper is not **primed**, but rather the whole plant is **stalk-cut** when it matures.

bruyere: See **briar**.

buey: Spanish for "ox," a *buey* is a castrated, domesticated bull used to plow fields and pull carts. *Bueyes* are still commonly used in cigar tobacco agriculture.

bulk: See **burro**.

bulldog: a pipe with an indentation carved into the circumference towards the top of the bowl. Bulldog pipes usually have a diamond-shaped stem.

bunch: the **filler** tobaccos which are rolled up with the **binder** leaf. After bunching and **pressing** the **wrapper** leaf is applied. The bunch is also called *enpuño* in Spanish.

bundle: a method of packaging cigars without a box, usually in groups of twenty-five or fifty. Bundles are typically used for less expensive cigars that may not have bands. Typically, cigar makers release their **seconds** in bundles.

burl: a hardened wood growth found on trees.

burl grain: a grain pattern found on smooth finish briar pipes that has tight, swirling patters; also referred to as "bird's eye."

burlap: strong, breathable material used to wrap filler and binder leaves for tobacco *añejamiento*.

Burley: light, air-cured tobacco that has a rich, nutty taste with slow, even burning qualities.

burros: in the context of the two stage fermentation model that TU teaches, burros are four to six foot tall piles of tobacco that constitute the most intense fermentation period. At critical temperature points, the *burros* are unraveled and re-piled to prevent burn out. In other contexts, the term can refer to any fermentation pile.

butane: a flavorless, natural gas made from petroleum, used in torch lighters. Butane is ideal for lighting luxury tobacco products. The best butane is filtered several times for optimal purity: quality matters when it comes to butane.

caballeria: unit of area used to measure land in Cuba, equivalent to 33.2 acres.

cabinet selection: cigars packaged in cedar boxes in lieu of paper wrapped boxes. These boxes provide direct contact with the cedar and may be preferable in long-term aging.

cabo: the Spanish (or Cuban-Spanish) term for a partially smoked and unlit cigar.

cake (pipe): the carbon that develops along the inner wall of the pipe chamber and acts as insulation for the bowl and promotes an even burn. Approximately 1/16" of cake is considered ideal for a pipe.

calabash (pipe): originally made from African gourds, traditionally trained by hand to grow into an "s" shape. Because the gourds are naturally fatter at one end, calabash pipes make for cool smoking instruments. The gourd cannot sustain extreme heat, so calabash pipes generally have a bowl insert made from ceramic, briar, or meerschaum. Today, the term calabash refers to any pipe in classic gourd "S" shape.

calumet (pipe): a decorated pipe made by Native Americans, commonly called a "peace pipe."

Cameroon: the common name for tobacco descended from Sumatran seed and grown in central Africa. Known for their rich flavors and aromas, Cameroon tobaccos are often used as wrapper leaves.

candela: also known as **double claro**, these leaves are **flue-cured** (or heat cured) to fix the chlorophyll levels in the leaf and produce the desired green color.

canoe: also canoeing; the uneven, one-sided burn of a cigar, caused by sub-standard rolling, improperly placed filler, uneven humidity, or poorly fermented raw materials.

cap: the circular piece of wrapper leaf that finishes the **head** of the cigar.

capa: a Spanish term for the cigar wrapper leaf.

capadura: a Spanish term for the second growth plant leaves. After the plant has been harvested/primed, the stalk is trimmed down and new leaves are allowed to grow. This process was common in Cuba where the farmers would allow the plant/leaves to re-grow and use those leaves for their own consumption. Capadura is especially common when growing *Pelo de Oro* tobacco varietals.

Capero No. 1: a newer Cuban dark tobacco varietal. Grown widely beginning in 2007, Capero No. 1 is a cross between Habanos 2000, Corojo '99 and Criollo '98. It produces an extra 2 to 3 leaves over other hybrids and has very large leaves. Capero No. 1 has been genetically engineered to produce no flowers and therefore no seeds: this will help Cuba maintain control over the plant's genetics where it is grown. The weakness of this hybrid is that the leaves have not held up well during fermentations.

capote: 1) a Spanish term for the cigar **binder** leaf; 2) a section of the **Criollo** plant used for fillers and binders.

carbonization (pipe): the process by which char changes to carbon and forms cake on the inside of the bowl. This carbonized material, cake, helps protect the briar from the inside out, keeps the bowl cool, and promotes an even smoking experience.

Carnauba: a wax derived from the palm of the Carnauba tree. This wax melts at high temperatures and is used to give pipes their final polish.

carotene: a naturally occurring organic compound found in some plants. When cigar tobacco is **air-cured**, the chlorophyll which gives the leaves their green color is broken down and the new yellow and orange carotene pigments are exposed.

carved (finish): a pipe that is sculpted and shaped by hand, see **freehand**.

Casa de Tabaco: a Spanish term for the curing barn which has open sides facing East and West for optimal air circulation. Tobacco is placed high up in the *Casa de Tobaco* after picking/priming to dry out and lose its chlorophyll.

casing: a top-coat of liquid flavoring that is added to pipe tobaccos (usually aromatics). Flavorings can include honey, liqueurs, extracts, etc.

Casquillo: the cylindrical instrument used to cut the round cigar caps from the tobacco leaf.

Catador: Spanish term for "taster"; *Catadores* ensure quality control by tasting batches of finished cigars.

CCST: Certified Cigar Sommelier Tobacconist, as defined and accredited by Tobacconist University. More specifically, an educated and trained cigar professional, usually working in restaurants, bars, and liquor stores. CCST specialize in cigar selection, presentation, and pairings.

CCT: Certified Consumer Tobacconist, as defined and accredited by Tobacconist University.

Cedar, Spanish: *Cedrela odorata*, Spanish Cedar is neither Spanish nor cedar; it is a member of the mahogany (*Meliaceae*) family. It is commonly used for cigar boxes and cigar aging because it is naturally pest resistant, **hygroscopic**, and naturally abundant in Central America and the Caribbean.

cedro: the Spanish term for Spanish Cedar (see **Cedar, Spanish**).

cello box: a cigar box with rounded sides. See **8-9-8**.

cellophane: a thin, transparent film made from regenerated cellulose, often used in the packaging of cigars.

cellulose: an insoluble substance derived from plant glucose; used as a binder in **homogenized tobacco leaf**.

centro fino: the third level of leaves from the top of the **corojo** plant, between the *centro gordo* and *centro ligero* leaves.

centro gordo: the second level of leaves from the top of the Corojo plant, just below the top corona leaves.

centro ligero: the leaves on the third level from the bottom of the corojo plant, between the *centro fino* and *uno y medio* leaves. Not to be confused with the **criollo** plant, where the term **ligero** refers to the top leaves, which are exposed to the most sun.

cepo: instrument used to measure the proper **ring gauge** of a finished cigar. This is usually a piece of wood with the appropriate size hole cut into it: the cigar is passed through to confirm it to the proper diameter.

Certified Cigar Reviews (CCR): the interactive web-based platform created by Tobacconist University where people can review and rate cigars using the Certified Tobacconist University standards and process.

Certified Cigar Sommelier Tobacconist (CCST): an educated and trained cigar professional, usually working in restaurants, bars, and liquor stores. CCST specialize in cigar selection, presentation, and pairings.

chamber (pipe): a chamber is the inside part of the bowl of a pipe where the tobacco is placed for smoking. Depending on the pipe, chambers vary in size, depth, and finish.

char: the partially scorched, pre-ash remnants of tobacco.

chaveta: a flat metal tool shaped like a half moon, and used to cut tobacco leaves by *torcedores* while rolling.

chemoreception: the process by which people (and other organisms) respond to chemical stimuli by using their sense of taste and smell.

Cheroot: one of the oldest known cigar shapes, from the Tamil *"curuttu,"* literally meaning "roll." The term usually refers to a mild and inexpensive cigar that tapers gradually from foot to head as is cut at both ends. Also referred to as a "**stogie**."

cherry pickers: consumers that scour retail tobacconists looking for hard-to-find products.

chinchal: popular during the 1800s, this term referred to small cigar factories in Cuba which manufactured cigars for domestic use.

chisel: *figurado* cigar with a round foot and a flattened/squared head.

chromolithography: the use of more than one color and stone (up to twenty-five) in lithography.

Churchill: a large format cigar, traditionally 7" x 47 ring gauge (rg).

churchwarden (pipe): a pipe shape with a long, curved stem, also known as a "yard of clay." Churchwardens were originally made of clay, and were enormously popular in Europe until the introduction of the briar pipe. Churchwardens tend to produce a cooler smoke due to the length the smoke has to travel from bowl to mouthpiece.

cigar: a cylinder of tobacco leaves rolled together; beginning in the center with filler tobaccos, bound with a binder leaf, and sheathed with a wrapper leaf. A premium cigar is made from only long leaf tobacco and is made by hand. The only exception might be "premium" cigars that are machine bunched but hand wrapped.

cigar maker: technically, this term could refer to a cigar roller, since they "make" cigars, or the factory owner who "makes" cigars. But, cigar maker is typically used in a much broader sense, referring to farmers, fermenters, blenders, and the people who put their names on a cigar brand.

cigar rolling table: a table distinguished by a partial shelf (approximately 40" high) over a standard table top (approximately 30" high). The partial top shelf creates extra space on top for placing finished cigars, while the space underneath hides the *goma*, *guillotina*, water, leaves, and other incidentals.

cigarette: finely shredded tobacco light tobaccos, wrapped in paper, smoked and inhaled for consumption. More importantly, the difference between cigars/pipe tobaccos and cigarettes is varietal, chemical, agricultural, processing, and usage—which impacts frequency of use.

cigarillo: a small, machine-made cigar composed of short filler tobacco. Cigarillos are often **dry-cured** and are not premium cigars since they are not made from long filler.

claro: a cigar wrapper leaf, pale to light brown in color. Claro leaves are grown under shade to keep their color light.

clay (pipe): a pipe made from hardened clay, popularized by Sir Walter Raleigh in the early 1600s, characterized by a small bowl and a long stem.

Clear Havana: a cigar made with Cuban tobacco in the United States, before the Cuban embargo.

cloud-grown: cigar tobacco grown in Ecuador which is naturally shaded by consistent cloud cover. The naturally diffused light diminishes vein size, yields thinner leaves with very consistent coloration, and a more subtle taste and aroma.

CMT: Certified Master Tobacconist, as defined and accredited by Tobacconist University.

Cohiba: 1) the cigar brand created for Fidel Castro in 1966; 2) the native Caribbean peoples' term for tobacco.

color (wrapper leaf): the general classifications of wrapper colors from lightest to darkest are: Double Claro, Claro, Colorado Claro, Colorado, Colorado Rosado, Colorado Maduro, Maduro, and Oscuro.

condensation irrigation: unique moisture produced (in the form of dew) in valleys during early morning hours and night.

condiment, tobacco: tobaccos like **Perique** and **Latakia** which are used in small portions to "spice" up blends.

contrast pairing: the process of pairing dissimilar flavors together to create an interplay which enhances the experience. Also see **pairing** and **like pairing**.

Copaneco: a variety of *Nicotiana* found growing wild in Honduras.

corncob (pipe): a traditional American pipe, the corncob's bowl is made from a dried and hollowed out cob with a reed or hollowed out piece of wood inserted for the stem and mouthpiece.

Corojo: one of the most famous and successful Cuban tobacco seed varietals, which is shade-grown and commonly used for cigar wrappers. From top to bottom, leaf classifications: Corona, Centro Gordo, Centro Fino, Centro Ligero, Uno Y Medio, and Libre de Pie.

Corona: 1) the top leaves of the Corojo plant; 2) a cigar 5½" long x 44 ring gauge.

Corona Gorda: a modern favorite cigar shape measuring 6" long x 50 ring gauge.

cosecha: Spanish for "harvesting."

country of origin (COO): the country where the cigar is manufactured; this rarely describes all of the components since cigars are often blended with tobaccos from different countries.

craftsman: a skilled worker who practices a trade or handicraft.

Criollo: a Cuban tobacco seed varietal grown under direct sunlight and used for fillers and binders. This varietal produces six to seven pairs of leaves, from top to bottom: Ligero, Seco, Volado, (all fillers) and Capotes (binders).

CRT: Certified Retail Tobacconist, as defined and accredited by Tobacconist University.

CST: Certified Salesforce Tobacconist, as defined and accredited by Tobacconist University.

Cuban seed: dark tobacco seeds that are descended from Cuban origins, but are now typically grown in other countries.

Cubatabaco: Cuban organization in charge of tobacco agriculture, processing, and production; from the 1960s to the mid-1990s.

cube cut: pipe tobacco that is cut or shredded into small, square pieces that are easily blended and smoked. Burley tobaccos are the most common cube cut.

cujes: long wooden lathes used to hold up pairs of tobacco leaves during **air curing** in *Casas de Tabaco*.

culebra: Spanish for "snake"; in this case describes the braiding of three loosely filled, thin cigars held together by string. The practice of braiding cigars together originated in Cuba as a means by which factory owners could control the rollers' cigar smoking. *Culebras* served as the workers' daily ration of cigars. As the rollers smoked the *culebras*, the squirmy look of the cigar signaled the factory managers that the rollers were not smoking premium inventory.

curing: the drying of raw (fresh-picked) tobacco. More precisely, curing is the process of altering the chemical and organic properties of the tobacco leaves, converting starch to sugar, oxidizing sugar, losing chlorophyll, moisture, etc. Freshly picked tobacco leaves contain as much as 85 percent of their weight in moisture. Once the moisture is removed, the chemical and organic changes of the curing process are halted. Different curing methods are used for different types of raw tobacco, namely air, fire, flue and sun-curing. See **dry-cured cigars** for information on the curing of finished cigars.

cut filler: see **short filler**.

dark tobaccos: the classification for tobaccos that are used to create cigars. Dark tobaccos are more robust than **light tobaccos**, which are used for **cigarettes** and pipe tobaccos.

date of creation (DOC): the date a cigar was manufactured.

default position: in the retail tobacconist's store, all objects have a physical location where they must be at any given time. While business can disrupt the look of a store, setting specific locations for fixtures, products, ashtrays and the like helps maintain a coherent merchandising strategy and organized facility.

dehumidification: the process of drying cigars. After the second fermentation, the filler and binder *gavillas* are laid on racks in climate controlled dehumidification rooms for several days to let the leaf recuperate and dry out. Dehumidification also occurs after the cigars have been rolled and placed in **marrying rooms**.

desbotonar: another form of pruning; the process of removing the flower buds before they bloom from the tobacco plants. This occurs at least one week prior to harvesting and prevents pollination (thereby preventing the plants from expending energy and resources on the flowers).

descriptors: words used to describe the flavors and sensations created by the tobacco and perceived by the taster.

deshijar: similar to pruning, *podar*, this process occurs in the fields on maturing plants. Smaller, non-viable leaves are removed to allow nutrients to flow to the larger leaves.

despalillar: Spanish for "stemming." Cigar wrappers have the entire stem removed, yielding two separate parts of the leaf to wrap cigars. Filler leaves have only half of the stem removed from the bottom of the leaf, creating a *"pata de rana"* ("frog's legs") shape.

diademas: a cigar approximately eight inches long and tapered at both ends, pointy at the head, with a bulge in the middle.

differentiation threshold: the **sensory threshold** where we can sense and perceive gradients in the tastes and smells (aromas) of a substance; lighter to heavier, milder to stronger.

dog rocket: slang for an unpalatable cigar.

dog walker: describes a smaller cigar which is ideal for the short amount of time it takes to walk a dog.

Double Claro: also known as Jade, **American Market Selection**, and *Candela*; leaves that have been flue- or heat-cured to fix the chlorophyll levels in the leaf, producing the desired green wrapper color.

Double Corona: a cigar approximately seven to eight inches long with a ring gauge (RG) of forty-nine or larger; larger than a **Churchill**.

double guillotine (cigar cutter): a cigar cutter with two straight blades locked in a frame, which makes a straight cut. A guillotine with one blade and two finger holes is a (single) guillotine, as a double guillotine must have two blades.

draw: the term used to describe how easily a cigar allows air to pass through it; e.g., a "loose" or a "tight" draw.

dry-cured cigars: cigars that are slowly baked in an oven after manufacturing. These cigars require only 12–15 percent relative humidity for preservation, approximately the same relative humidity as in a home. Popular and manufactured in Europe, dry cured cigars are usually machine-made with Sumatran, Central African, and/or Brazilian tobaccos.

Dublin (pipe): a pipe with a half-oval shaped bowl; this format may have either a bent or straight stem.

Ebonite: a brand name for a hard rubber used in making pipe stems, originally developed to mimic ebony wood.

ebouchon: the briar burl in its most raw, post-harvest shape; ebouchons are purchased by pipe makers, dried, and stored until they are ready to be carved into pipes.

electronic cigarette: also known as e-cigarettes, these are electronic products which vaporize liquid nicotine and simulate the look and effects of cigarette smoking. The vapor is not smoke, but rather a water mist which momentarily resembles smoke.

enbetunando: the wetting down of tobacco with **betun**, a mixture of water and tobacco residues, to accelerate the fermentation process.

encallado: a method for growing cigar tobaccos that utilizes vertical tents or cloths as windbreaks.

English blend (pipe tobacco): also referred to as **Balkan**, English blends are composed of **Oriental**, **Virginia**, **Latakia**, and **Perique** tobaccos.

English Cigarette blend: a cigarette blend consisting almost entirely of flue-cured tobacco, also referred to as **Virginia**. English blend cigarettes tend to have a fuller flavor than **American blends**.

English Market Selection (EMS): refers to cigars which have light to medium brown wrapper color—popularized in England during the twentieth century.

enpuño: Spanish for "bunch" or "fist"; denotes both the **bunch** as well as where and how the bunch is held by the **roller**.

entubado bunching (*entubar*): a rolling format in which each filler leaf is rolled into itself then bunched with other individually rolled leaves. *Entubado* bunching/rolling, the most complex and difficult rolling method, and therefore the rarest, creates a more firmly packed and balanced cigar by providing an excellent draw.

epidemiology: the branch of medical science that studies factors affecting the health and illness of populations. The statistics and results of epidemiological studies and used as the reasoning/logic for public health and public policy decision making and legislation.

escaparte: also known as an *añejamiento* room; Spanish for the aging cabinet or room where cigars are stored and **married** after rolling.

escogida: Cuban term for "the selection." In Cuban farming villages, the *escogida* is a ritual and festival held while the tobacco leaf crop is graded and selected by factory representatives. *Escogida* can also refer to the color classification system for leaves and the room where this occurs.

estate vintage: refers to a specific year's crop from a specific farm or "estate." See **vintage**.

estrujado **bunching**: a hybrid of *entubado* bunching, also known as "lazy *entubado*." This technique uses a base of two tobacco leaves which are folded (semi-scrolled) and the filler leaves are scrolled and placed within it. Lastly, the entire bunch is wrapped with the binder leaf.

ETS: environmental tobacco smoke, also known as secondhand smoke (SHS).

evaporation humidification: a humidifier that utilizes the evaporative qualities of water; typically, the surface area of the humidifier is proportionate to the size of the box and releases water at a rate that creates a relative humidity of 70 to 73 percent.

exhausting: the expulsion of heat and **ammonia** from the tobacco leaf during **fermentation**.

fabrica: a Cuban term for a cigar factory.

facing: the proper way to display a cigar, with the head facing up and the band facing forward. The term also refers to all merchandise since most products have a "face" and should be properly displayed.

fermentation: also known as "sweating" or "*trabajando*"; the natural, vigorous, and highly controlled process that accounts for the majority of taste and aroma development in cigar tobaccos. Fermentation occurs when moisture, heat, oxygen, and pressure reach optimal levels resulting in the expulsion of ammonia and other unpalatable components of the leaf. The temperatures in fermentation piles are closely monitored and regulated through deconstruction and reconfiguration to prevent overheating. Over-fermentation will ruin the taste and aroma of tobacco. On the other hand, under-fermented tobacco is noxious, unrefined, and "green" (a term describing flavor, not leaf color).

ferrule (pipe): a decorative ring, usually metal, used to reinforce the wood around the end of the **shank**.

figurado: any cigar that is not a *parejo*; also known as shaped cigars; e.g., **torpedo**, **pyramid**, or **perfecto**.

filete: narrow strips of paper used to seal the edges/border of cigar boxes.

fill (pipe): pits or imperfections in briar can be filled in with wood putty or some other reparative compound. Typically, a fill is visible to the human eye because it does not look like the surrounding briar. While fills are common on many pipes, a high grade briar pipe should be rejected or downgraded if fill is used.

filler: the combination of distinct tobacco leaves that constitute the "guts" of the cigar. Filler must be expertly **bunched** to make a well-constructed cigar that will both draw and burn well. See *tripa*.

finca: Spanish for "farm."

finish: a tasting term; describes the lingering flavors left behind on the smoker's palate.

fire-curing: a curing process that uses small fires in an enclosed space to flavor tobaccos. Fire-curing involves using aromatic woods as fuel, imparting flavor to the tobaccos. Fire-curing can be done after sun-curing, as is the case for **Latakia** tobaccos.

flag: a small piece of the leaf trimmed to close the head of the cigar during cigar wrapping.

flake cut: pipe tobacco that has been pressed into blocks and then sliced into thin, broad, flat flakes. Flake cuts must be rubbed out before smoking.

flame grain: a grain pattern found on smooth finish briar pipes that has narrowing or widening streaks that mimic flame.

flat top: a cigar box designed to hold twenty-five cigars with twelve on the bottom and thirteen on top; also called a thirteen-topper.

flavor: combination of taste (mouth) and aroma (nose).

flavor memory: the ability to recall specific flavors (tastes and aromas) in your mind.

flue-curing: a curing process that applies high levels of heat to tobaccos in an enclosed space. The heat dries out the leaves and fixes the sugar content of the tobacco. This technique is most commonly used on Virginia varietals which have naturally high sugar levels.

foot: the flat and open end of a cigar; the part of the cigar that is lit.

format: see *vitola*

fortaleza: the Spanish term that can describe cigar strength and vigor. *Fortaleza* can also refer to the overall sensory input (robustness) from a cigar, not just strength as it relates to **nicotine**.

freehand: also known as sculpted, freestyle, or carved, a freehand pipe is not a basic or classic pipe shape; rather, it is carved to high-light the best features of the briar or grain.

fuma: 1) Spanish name given to a quality control committee that smokes and tests cigars; 2) a *fuma* can also be a short filler, rusti-cally finished cigar that may include a twisted head and a shaggy foot.

fumo: a traditional Cuban term for a cigar with an unfinished "shaggy" foot and a twisted head and cap.

galera: Spanish for "galley"; the workroom where cigars are hand rolled.

gavilla: also known as a "hand"; bunches of tobacco leaves held together by string to organize the tobacco for fermentation and *añejamiento*.

German blend (cigarette): similar to an American blend, but uses more Oriental tobacco. These cigarettes have a milder taste since the tobacco is not as heavily cased and flavored as American cigarettes.

goma: Spanish for "gum"; a vegetable gum; this is a natural adhe-sive used to seal the cigar leaves and wrapper at the head.

grain disruption: a change in grain from straight/flame/burl or no grain (bald spot) to another pattern. Grain disruptions are common on many extraordinary pipes, but a briar pipe with only one grain pattern and no disruption is rare and spectacular.

guajiro: Spanish; a Cuban agricultural worker and/or peasant.

guillotina: the cutting instrument used by the *torcedore* to trim the foot of the cigar after it has been rolled.

guillotine: a cigar cutter with a straight blade locked in a frame designed to cut off a thin slice of the closed cigar head.

gum: see *goma*.

gustation: the act or sense of tasting with the mouth/tongue.

H.T.F.: "Hard-to-Find"; an acronym popularized among Internet cigar communities for limited edition or special release cigars.

Habano: a cigar rolled in Cuba, exclusively from Cuban tobacco leaves.

Habanos S.A.: the joint venture between the Cuban government, Cubatabaco, and the European firm, Altadis. Habanos S.A. controls the worldwide distribution and marketing of Cuban cigars. Habanos S.A. owns the trademarks for all Cuban cigar brands outside of the US.

Habano seed: a traditional Cuban seed varietal family that has been hybridized and cross-bred to create many new modern varietals. Traditional Habano seed is still used to produce many cigars throughout Central America and the Caribbean.

half-wheel: see *media rueda*.

hand: see *gavilla.*

hand-rolled: a cigar made exclusively by human hands.

handicraft: a trade requiring manual skills.

harvesting: the process of picking tobacco leaves from the plant; see **priming**.

Havana: 1) the capital of Cuba; 2) a cigar rolled in Cuba exclusively from Cuban tobacco.

Havana-obsessed consumers: Since Cuba is the "birthplace" of cigar tobacco, many consumers believe that Cuban cigars are the best in the world. While this sentiment has changed dramatically since the 1990s, there are still many cigar smokers who believe in Cuban cigar supremacy. This bias is further exacerbated by the US trade embargo against Cuba that makes Cuban cigars difficult to acquire in the USA.

head: the cap and shoulder of a cigar; the end of the cigar that touches the mouth.

hecho a mano: Spanish for "made by hand"; may refer to cigars that have machine bunched filler.

herf: slang; 1) describes the act of drawing on a cigar; 2) a gathering of cigar lovers expressly for the consumption of cigars.

Homogenized Tobacco Leaf (H.T.L.): a smokable tobacco composite of reconstituted tobacco leaf mixed with stems and cellulose. Originally developed by General Cigar in the 1950s, H.T.L. is not a component of premium cigars and pipe tobaccos but helped to expand the machine-made cigar industry by creating cheaper alternatives.

hookah: also *narghile, narghila, nargile, nargila, sheesha, shisha*, water-pipe, or hubbly-bubbly; an indirect smoking system that passes the smoke through water or other liquid before it is delivered to the smoker's mouth.

hot: any tobacco that is transferring heat to the palate. This can be caused by smoking too quickly, or by improper cigar rolling or pipe packing. Tobacco that burns hot is not combusting at the proper rate and must be allowed to cool down.

humidifier: an apparatus that generates and maintains the 65 to 73 percent relative humidity needed to keep cigars optimally conditioned. Note: distilled water or the closest alternative should be used in humidifiers as minerals and other contaminants can clog the **hygroscopic** medium and/or taint cigars.

humidistat: a device used to regulate humidity through a humidifier.

humidor: any container intended to store cigars at the appropriate humidity; usually a sealed box or container that can maintain a constant 70 percent **relative humidity**.

hygrometer: an instrument that measures relative humidity. Analog models need to be calibrated immediately after purchase while most digital hygrometers are factory calibrated.

hygroscopic: the quality of ready absorption and retention of humidity in a given substance. Cigars and tobacco are hygroscopic by nature and require proper humidity to live and thrive properly.

I.P.C.P.R.: currently known as the Premium Cigar Association (PCA), the International Premium Cigar and Pipe Retailers association was founded in 1932 as the R.T.D.A.; this is the premier organization for retail tobacconists.

igloodor: also "coolerdor"; a makeshift humidor made from a plastic cooler. This method of cigar storage is inexpensive but has drawbacks for long-term storage as plastic containers do not have the hygroscopic qualities of Spanish Cedar and the tight seal inhibits air circulation in the humidor, increasing the risk of over-humidification and mold. Extra care and monitoring may be needed to maintain cigars in this type of humidor.

Jalapa Valley: a famous cigar tobacco growing area in the North Eastern part of Nicaragua, near the Southern border of Honduras.

Jamastran Valley: a famous cigar tobacco growing area in the South Eastern part of Honduras near the Northern Nicaraguan border.

knocker (pipe): a (typically cork) device that rests in an ashtray and helps pipe smokers empty their bowl by knocking the pipe rim against it.

label (cigar): the main decorative paper glued onto cigar boxes.

large cigars: cigars weighing more than three pounds per one thousand cigars as defined by the US government.

Latakia: sun-, then fire-cured Oriental tobaccos. The use of aromatic woods and fragrant herbs in the fire curing process impart a smoky quality. Too strong and spicy to be smoked alone, Latakia enhances and distinguishes other blends.

leaf: the part of the tobacco plant meant to be smoked.

lector: in Cuba, a traditional professional who reads newspapers and books to the cigar rollers throughout the work day.

leverage: the use of a tool or force to gain an advantage including the use of words, relationships, knowledge, experience, body language, humor, etc.

libre de pie: Spanish for "free feet"; the two leaves at the base of the **Corojo** plant.

Lieberman (bunch) rolling: a rolling technique that uses the Lieberman machine to bunch and bind tobacco filler leaves. Commonly used today in premium cigar factories across the world, cigars bunched using the Lieberman machine still usually have hand applied wrappers.

liga: Spanish for **blend**; the combination of different tobacco leaves and proportions to create a specific character and taste. In a cigar, this includes the filler, binder, and wrapper leaves.

ligador: Spanish for "master blender" in a cigar factory.

ligero: one of the three basic types of filler leaves from the **Criollo** plant (the other two being **seco** and **volado**). From the top of the plant, ligero leaves are exposed to the most sun and renowned for being dense, rich, and robust.

light tobaccos: the classification for tobaccos that are used to create **cigarettes** and pipe tobaccos. The varietals in this category are less robust than the **dark tobaccos** used to make cigars.

like pairing: the process of pairing food and beverages with cigars that share similar flavor traits. Also see **pairing** and **contrast pairing**.

lip (pipe): surrounding the air hole and being located just above the bit, the part of the stem which flares open slightly to allow the teeth a place to rest.

lithography: the process of carving an image onto a flat stone and using pigments to replicate said image, in reverse, onto paper.

little cigars: cigars weighing three pounds or less per thousand, as defined by the US government.

long filler: the whole leaves which are used in premium cigars: not chopped up pieces of leaf or **HTL**.

lonsdale: a long, slender cigar, usually around 6" by 42 ring gauge.

Lucite (pipe stem): a trade name for a type of hard, durable plastic polymer commonly used for pipe **stems**. Although a bit hard on the teeth, Lucite stems retain their finish over long periods and are easily polished.

luxury tobacco: tobacco products which are created by master craftsmen utilizing premium quality tobacco and intended to be enjoyed while savoring your time. Luxury tobacco is never homogenized, commoditized, or used out of habit or addiction.

M.Y.O.: acronym for Make Your Own cigarettes.

machine made: refers to cigars that have been wrapped and bunched by machines. These are not premium cigars.

maduro: in its most limited sense, the term maduro can simply refer to a dark or black **wrapper** color—these color wrappers can result from late **primings** or **stalk-cutting broadleaf** tobaccos. But, a true maduro will have a wrapper which has undergone longer and/or more intense (higher temperature) fermentation that produces a richer, earthier, and sweeter flavor.

magnesium: an element, found in soil, that affects ash whiteness and density. Too much magnesium in the soil produces ash flaking.

manojo: a bundle of four *gavillas*.

manzana: a Latin American unit of measure equivalent to approximately 1.7 acres of land; its precise measure may vary from country to country.

marrying room: the room in which cigars, bound in bundles of fifty, are stored in cedar cabinets after rolling. The room and cabinets allow the cigars to lose some of their excessive humidity and reach a balanced state. This process is necessary because cigar tobacco is exceptionally moist during rolling.

Mata Fina: a Brazilian varietal of cigar tobacco that is sun grown in the Reconcavo Basin. It produces excellent **oscuro** and **maduro** wrappers. The flavor profile is typically rich, mild to medium in strength, very aromatic, and naturally sweet.

maturation: the point at which tobacco leaves are ready for priming; at maturation, the leaves lay horizontally, the center vein has a yellowish color, and they cut away freely.

mazo: Spanish term; a bundle of twenty-five, or more commonly fifty, cigars.

media rueda: Spanish term meaning "half wheel"; a bundle of fifty cigars.

Meerschaum: German term meaning "sea foam"; a light, clay-like mineral that is primarily found in Turkey, resembling ivory. Meerschaum has become synonymous for the intricately carved pipes that are created from it.

Meerschaum (pipe): pipes carved from **meerschaum** which are renowned for their intricate carvings.

merchandising: the physical and visual language with which displayed products communicate with the customer: it should be commensurate with the quality of the product and the store.

mojo: the thorough wetting of *gavillas*/tobacco leaves.

mold, cigar: a fungus that appears as a woolly growth found on damp and/or decaying organic matter, rendering the cigars un-smokable.

molds: wood or plastic forms that give the binder and the filler their cigar-like shape. Cigar molds are filled with bunches and then placed in a press for approximately forty-five minutes and then rotated by one-third, several times, to eliminate any seams. The bunches can also be left in the mold and press overnight.

mortise: the hole carved into the shank of the pipe, into which the **tenon** is fit, connecting the bowl to the mouthpiece.

mouthfeel: 1) the general sensation of the unlit cigar wrapper in the mouth. 2) the sensation in the mouth created by the **body** (fullness, richness, or thinness) of the smoke of a tobacco.

MSA (Master Settlement Agreements): see **TSA**.

MSRP (Manufacturer Suggested Retail Price): while a suggestion, these are rarely useful since state taxes vary throughout the US.

natural (wrapper color): term describing a light brown wrapper color; ranging from **Claro** to **Colorado Rosado**.

Natural Cavendish: pipe tobacco that is steamed, usually with sugars or flavoring in the water, and pressed for an additional curing/fermentation period. Natural Cavendish differs from Black Cavendish in that it goes through a less vigorous pressing, yielding a milder flavor.

navy cut: also known as a navy plug, given the name because sailors would fill a long canvas tube with tobacco and flavorings (rum, fruits, spices), then twist the tube tight, mimicking the **pressing**

process. This technique created a dense rope of tobacco about an inch thick from which plugs were sliced off. Tobacco prepared in this manner must be **rubbed out** to be smokable.

Nicotiana: a genus of plants containing approximately sixty species, most of which are found in the Americas. Of the fourteen species found in North America, nine were used by Native Americans for various purposes; two of those nine were consumed by smoking, *Nicotiana rustica* and *Nicotiana tabacum*.

Nicotiana rustica: one of approximately sixty species of *Nicotiana*. During the **Pre-Columbian** era, *N. rustica* was popular among indigenous North Americans, prior to the arrival of *N. tabacum* from Central and South America. *N. rustica* contains twenty times more nicotine than *N. tabacum*. Although *N. rustica* represents only a small fraction of global tobacco production today, its use and commercial production is well documented into the seventeenth century.

Nicotiana tabacum: tobacco; the most famous species in the *Nicotiana* family, *N. tabacum* is the largest cash crop on earth and is found exclusively as a cultivated species. *N. tabacum* does not grow in the wild.

nicotine: a naturally occurring **biphasic**, organic compound in the same family of substances as caffeine. Nicotine is found in tobacco plants and to a lesser degree in tomatoes, green peppers, potatoes, and eggplant.

nitrogen: an element found in soil that increases root growth, nicotine content, plant yield, leaf width and luster.

non-aromatic: a pipe tobacco to which no additional flavoring/ **casing** has been added. This term is something of a misnomer since these, like all tobaccos, produce aromas.

nub: the last one to two inches of a cigar; may refer to "smoking past the band."

nubbing: the act of smoking the last inch or two of a cigar, or "smoking past the band."

nutrient erosion: a result of the topography of valleys that allows nutrients to flow over time from surrounding hills and mountains into the valley.

oil: exuded by tobacco leaves as they age, oils are the result of well-conditioned cigars.

olfaction: 1) the sense of smell; 2) the act of smelling.

Olor: the Spanish term for "smell"; a variety of Dominican cigar tobacco that has large leaves commonly used in filler and binder. Olor tobacco can have a distinctly dry flavor or a drying effect on the mouth.

organoleptic: being, affecting or relating to qualities such as taste, odor, color, and the feel of a substance that stimulates the senses.

Oriental: tobacco grown mostly in Southern Europe and the Middle East; this plant has relatively small leaves and produces fragrant, dry flavor profiles with low nicotine and sugar content. Oriental tobacco is typically **primed**, **sun-cured,** and **fermented**.

orthonasal olfaction: smelling odors that travel directly through the nose to the olfactory nerves; e.g., wafting cigar/pipe smoke under the nose.

oscuro: the blackest shade of tobacco leaf, but not necessarily a **maduro**. Typically Mexican and Brazilian Broadleaf varietals can achieve this color without going through the additional maduro fermentation.

P.C.A: Premium Cigar Association, formerly known as International Premium Cigar and Pipe Retailers association (IPCPR). Founded in 1932 as the Retail Tobacco Dealers of America (RTDA), this is the premier trade organization for retail tobacconists in the USA.

pairing: the art and practice of combining beverages, food, occasions, and events with cigars in order to enhance the organoleptic experience. Also see **contrast pairing** and **like pairing**.

palate: 1) literally, the roof of the mouth; 2) a personal preference concerning **taste**; 3) the sense of taste.

panatela: a slender cigar shape, traditionally 6" x 38 ring gauge, though frequently longer.

parejo: straight sided cigars; also known as standard or straight cigars, as opposed to **figurado** cigars.

passive humidifier: a passive humidifier has no electrical or moving parts and works on simple evaporative and chemical equilibrium principles. Passive humidifiers are intended for smaller humidification needs and commonly used in travel and desktop humidors.

Pelo de Oro: this is a Spanish term meaning "golden hair." It refers to a potent Cuban cigar varietal which was popular in the early and middle 1900s. This tobacco could be used for wrapper and filler as well, but it is disease prone and can infest entire crops and regions so it is rarely grown today. *Pelo de Oro* can be considered a *campesino* or *guajiro* tobacco since many agricultural workers grow and smoke it to this day—especially in the central part of Cuba. It is known for being quite strong and flavorful as well as sweet.

perfecto: a cigar approximately four to six inches long, tapered at both ends, with a rounded head and bulbous at the center.

Perique: a **Burley** tobacco grown only in St. James Parish, Louisiana. Perique is air-cured then fermented in oak barrels to produce an extremely robust tobacco with high nicotine levels. Perique is primarily used as a **condiment** in pipe tobacco blends and occasionally in cigarettes.

picadura: 1) Spanish term for "short filler," or scraps of tobacco; 2) small, underdeveloped leaves that grow just under the tobacco flower and above the ligero/corona leaves. The Spanish term "*pica dura*" translates as "bites hard/strong."

piercer: also called a lance, a cutter used to poke small holes through the head of a cigar.

pig-tail: a cigar head finishing technique that rolls the flag into a tight scroll then ties it into a knot. Pig-tails can easily be bitten off in lieu of cutting.

pilone: in the context of the two stage fermentation model taught by Tobacconist University, a one to three foot tall pile of tobacco in which the initial fermentation occurs. Today, in countries like Honduras and the Dominican Republic, *pilone* can refer to any fermentation pile.

Piloto: a varietal family of filler tobacco that originated in Cuba but is now commonly cultivated in the Dominican Republic and Central America.

pinch test (pipe tobacco): a method for evaluating pipe tobacco's fitness for smoking and/or storage. Take a small clump of pipe tobacco between the thumb and forefinger and gently squeeze it together. If it makes a crackling sound or breaks, it is probably too dry to smoke and definitely too dry for storing or aging. If it sticks together for more than a few seconds, it is too moist for smoking, storing, or aging.

pipe: a device used for smoking, usually consisting of a tube connecting a mouthpiece to a bowl.

pit: also known as a "sand pit"; a naturally occurring concave depression in the briar. Pits are found on all briar, so even extraordinary pipes may have a pit or two. If the pit is not too large, the pipe maker may leave it exposed and not fill it in. Usually, only close scrutiny will reveal these minor blemishes.

plancha: Spanish for "iron"; the wooden boards on which tobacco leaves are placed before fermentation.

plug: an obstruction in the draw of a cigar, resulting from poor craftsmanship or inferior raw materials.

plug (cut): a slice of tobacco from a dense, rope-like blend. See **navy cut**.

plume: also known as bloom; a naturally occurring byproduct of cigar aging. As the cigar exudes oils through the wrapper, the oils crystallize on the outside and form a white powder-like substance. Plume can be wiped off with no negative consequences.

podar: Spanish for "pruning"; the process of trimming down seedlings while they are still in the *semilleros*. By cutting off between half and two-thirds of each tobacco leaf, agronomists force the plant to spend its energy on root and stalk development instead of on the leaves.

poker (pipe): 1) a pipe with a cylindrical, flat bottomed bowl; 2) a slender piece of metal that is used to aerate and loosen tobacco in a pipe bowl as well as clear the pipe's air hole.

popular: a Cuban term for a cigar made exclusively for the local Cuban market and not exported.

pot (pipe): a **billiard** shaped pipe, but with a shorter bowl.

potassium: an element found in soil; has an important relationship to the burn rate of tobacco.

pre-carbonized (pipe): a finish applied to the **briar bowl** chamber which intends to mimic the effects of **carbonization**.

Pre-Columbian: refers to the period of American history prior to the arrival of Christopher Columbus. More loosely, the term may apply to all time before and until indigenous peoples of the Americas made contact with Europeans.

pre-light: the term used to describe the characteristics of a tobacco before it is lit and smoked.

premium cigar: made only from natural, long leaf tobacco and crafted by hand.

press, cigar: an apparatus that exerts pressure on cigar **molds**, compressing the tobacco into a cylindrical shape.

pressed tobacco: pipe tobacco contained under pressure exerted by a machine. Pressing for hours or days can help different tobacco flavors marry as well as create a manageable brick that can be packaged, aged, and/or **flake cut**. Under the proper conditions, long-term pressing, as done with **Cavendish** tobaccos, can lead to **fermentation**, dramatically changing and developing the tobacco.

priming: harvesting premium tobacco two or three leaves at a time, approximately once a week. The process starts at the bottom of the plant and continues upward, allowing the top leaves to get more sun and reach optimal maturation before being picked; the higher the priming, the stronger the tobacco.

propylene glycol (PG): organic, liquid alcohol that mixes well with water in any proportion. PG is used in **reverse osmosis** humidification systems to assist in regulating humidity levels in humidors; mostly, it inhibits water evaporation.

punch: a cigar cutter consisting of a small, circular blade intended to pierce a round hole in the head of a cigar. Sometimes referred to as a "bullet" or "bull's eye."

puro: describes a cigar in which all the tobacco comes from the same country. *Puro* can also be a generic Spanish term used to describe any cigar.

Puro Integritas: the Tobacconist University motto; it is a hybrid of Spanish, Latin, and double entendre, Puro Integritas refers to "Pure Integrity" and "Cigar Integrity."

pyramid: also *pyramide* and *piramide*; a cigar that is tapered to a point at the head and blossoms toward the cylindrical foot.

quisqueyas: the Spanish word used in the Dominican Republic for *casas de tabaco* or **air-curing** barns.

R.T.D.A.: Retail Tobacco Dealers of America, the former name of the **I.P.C.P.R.** and **P.C.A.**

R.Y.O.: Roll Your Own; pertaining to cigarettes, these tobaccos are usually shag cut for easy rolling and smoking. See **M.Y.O.**

random grain: a grain pattern that is not uniform; this may include a combination of straight, flame, burl/bird's eye, and/or bald spots where no distinguished pattern is present.

ready rubbed: **flake cut** pipe tobacco that has been broken up prior to packaging.

reamer: a pipe tool used to clean out excess char from the bowl and facilitate an even **cake**. Pipe reamers are shaped fit inside the **chamber** and spread out to apply even pressure along the interior walls. When turned, they remove char and compress existing cake.

recognition threshold: the sensory threshold where we are able to sense specific tastes and smells.

Reconstituted Tobacco Sheet: R.T.S.; developed by R. J. Reynolds in the 1930s, R.T.S. is comprised of stems, leaf, cellulose, additives, flavorings, and ingredients that are formed into sheets of "paper" and then shredded to be used in cigarette manufacturing.

relative humidity: the measure of humidity expressed as a percentage of the moisture content in the air. Ideal humidity for long-term preservation of cigars is 70 percent RH.

Remedios: a tobacco growing region in central Cuba which includes *Cienfuegos*, *Santa Clara*, and *Sancti Spiritus* provinces.

retro-haling: the act of moving smoke from the back of the mouth, up through the sinuses, and exhaling through the nasal passages.

In order to retro-hale, the mouth and sinuses can be connected by making a "gulping" action and exhaling through the nose at the same time. Retro-haling creates a powerful synergy of **taste** and **olfaction** (aroma/smell) where the spices/notes, body, flavor (taste+smell), and intensity of the cigar will be pronounced simultaneously.

retronasal olfaction: the act of sensing odors that originate from substances in the mouth; see **retro-haling**.

reverse osmosis humidification: a humidification process that utilizes propylene glycol (PG) and water to create the desired humidity. PG primarily acts as a buffer in the humidifier so that water is not released too quickly.

ribbon cut: pipe tobacco cut into thin, long ribbons. This cut is shorter and thicker than a **shag cut**.

ring gauge (RG): a unit of measure that describes the diameter of the cigar in sixty-fourths of an inch in North America; in Cuba and Europe, ring gauge is measured in millimeters.

robusto: a contemporary American favorite **vitola**, the size is approximately 5" x 50 ring gauge (RG).

rosado: Spanish term meaning "reddish"; refers to cigar wrappers that have a brown-red tint.

roto: Spanish term meaning "broken"; refers to damaged or broken wrapper leaves after they are sorted.

Royal Palm: *Roystonea regia*, also known as the Cuban Royal Palm, grows between forty and fifty feet, its leaves are commonly used for roofing tobacco barns and its bark for making *tercios*.

rubbing out: the process of breaking up a dense tobacco in the palm of the hand. Place tobacco in one palm and apply gentle pressure to the tobacco with the other palm while moving your hands in small, circular motions. This will loosen and break up the tobacco enough to prepare it for smoking. Rubbing out is typically necessary with flake and plug tobaccos.

rusticated finish: a deliberately roughened external surface on a briar. This process produces a more sophisticated finish than sandblasting because it is achieved through more tedious hand tooling.

sabroso: the Spanish word for **savory**; it also means "tasty."

San Andreas Negro: the most famous Mexican cigar varietal grown in the San Andreas Valley, San Andreas Negro was traditionally a **stalk-cut** tobacco, which produces excellent binder and **maduro** wrappers. Due to the toughness and resilience of the leaf, it holds up well during the extra **fermentation** required to produce maduro wrappers.

San Vincente: a varietal family now widely grown in the Dominican Republic. This cigar tobacco is commonly used for filler and binder; San Vincente varietals are a little lighter than **Piloto** and can have a mouthwatering effect and be a little acidic; they are not as dry as **Olor** varietals.

sandblast finish: a briar pipe finishing technique which utilizes compressed air and sand or other particulate to remove excess wood from the pipe. The result is textured, rustic finish.

savory: the taste sensation produced by **umami**. The Spanish word equivalent is *sabroso*. More generally, savory can be something that is pleasing to the sense of taste, by way of seasoning, that is not characteristically sweet.

scissor, cigar: unlike regular scissors, these scissors are shaped specifically to make a precise cut to the head of the cigar.

scraper, pipe: a spoon-like pipe tool used to remove excess char from the pipe chamber. Scrapers can potentially damage the cake, making reamers the more preferred tool for this task.

seasoning: the process of slowly raising the moisture level in a humidor until the desired humidity is reached.

seco: filler tobacco leaves from the center of the **Criollo** plant. For other varietals, seco can refer to the lower **primings**. Seco leaves are valued for their moderate flavor and good burning qualities; they are not as thick as **Ligero** or as light as **Volado**.

second (cigars): cigars that have not met the aesthetic or construction standards of the manufacturer and are sold un-banded and without boxes.

seed families: the five major cigar seed varietal families are Mata Fina, Broadleaf, Habanesis (Habano), Sumatra, and San Andres. All contemporary seed varietals originate from one of these families.

semilleros: nurseries where seeds germinate for approximately forty-five days before being transplanted to the fields.

sensory thresholds: the limits at which our physiological senses recognize a sensation. In order for people to sense a substance through taste or smell, it must be present in sufficient concentrations. Also see **absolute, terminal, recognition**, and **differentiation** thresholds.

shade-grown: tobacco, typically wrappers, grown under cheesecloth (*tapados*) to minimize the harsh rays of the sun. Shade-grown tobaccos have a more uniform appearance and a subtler and delicate flavor. Shade-grown leaves are also a little thinner and more elastic than **sun-grown** leaves.

shag cut: tobacco that is finely cut or shredded into long threads that are thinner and longer than a **ribbon cut**. Virginia tobaccos lend themselves to this cut because of their large size. This cut is common for natural **R.Y.O.** cigarette tobaccos as well.

shaggy foot: when the wrapper leaf is left un-trimmed on the foot of the cigar. This shaggy wrapper can be removed or lit to start the cigar.

shank (pipe): part of the pipe's bowl and carved from the same **ebouchon** or block of **meerschaum**. The shank contains the air hole and connects the bowl to the stem.

shisha: also *sheesha*; tobacco used for hookah smoking. Shisha is typically pre-moistened with water, honey and/or molasses and flavored with fruit and/or spices. Shisha is too moist to smoke with a simple flame, so it must be kept lit by placing a hot coal on top of it.

short filler: the chopped up pieces of tobacco used as filler in non-premium cigars. Short filler burns quicker and with far less complexity than **long filler** leaf.

shoulder: the rounded curve that transitions from the body to the head of a cigar. After properly cutting the head of a cigar, some shoulder should remain to keep the cigar from unraveling.

SHS: Secondhand Smoke, also known as Environmental Tobacco Smoke (ETS).

smemory: a word coined by Tobacconist University to emphasize the strong connections between human olfaction/smell, memory and emotions.

smokerism: belief or actions that presuppose nonsmokers are morally or ethically superior to smokers. Since the latter part of the twentieth century, smokerism has become a pervasive, global trend.

smoking: the act of tasting and savoring the flavors and sensations produced by burning luxury and premium tobaccos.

smooth (finish): a briar pipe that has been sanded and polished to reveal the grain as much as possible; smooth briars can be naturally treated or dyed with stain to achieve a variety of shades and colors.

snuff: a ground up, powder-like tobacco that is inhaled or "snuffed." Snuffing tobacco was popularized in Europe. In America, snuff can refer to dipping tobacco which is placed in the mouth, between the gums and mouth wall; also, see **snus**.

snus: like snuff (and dip), snus is powderized tobacco that is placed between the lip and gums. Popular in Sweden and Norway, this type of snuff is typically steam or **flue-cured**, not **fermented**, and contains no added sugar. Snus use typically does not require spitting. It is illegal in the European Union, except in Norway and Sweden.

Sommelier: an educated and trained wine professional, usually working in restaurants, bars and liquor stores. Sommeliers specialize in wine selection, presentation, and pairings.

S.O.T.L.: acronym for "Sisters of the Leaf."

Spanish Cedar: see **Cedar, Spanish**.

spice: a physical sensation that varies from tingling to stinging in the mouth, back of the throat, palate, throughout our nasal passages and nose.

spill: Cedar strips used for lighting cigars. These can be procured from the Spanish Cedar dividers used to separate rows of cigars in boxes.

spot carved (finish/pipe): spot carving normally refers to a hand-carved decorative accent on a pipe, but it is usually employed to cover up a flaw in the briar.

stalk-curing: the process of air curing tobacco leaves while they are still attached to the stalk. Stalk-Curing can be applied to **Stalk-Cut** or **Stalk-Primed** tobaccos. This process takes longer and is more expensive than traditional air-curing but it nourishes the leaves with nutrients from the stalk—creating an extraordinary end product.

stalk-cut: a plant which is harvested all at once by cutting the stalk, low to the ground. Unlike **primed** plant leaves, the stalk and all of the leaves are harvested at one time. This technique is common with **Broadleaf** and **San Andreas Negro** tobaccos that are typically used for **maduro** and **oscuro** color wrappers.

stalk-priming: as with **priming**, this process involves harvesting approximately a pair of leaves per week, but starts at the top and works down the plant. In addition, leaves are picked with a small piece of the stalk intact, holding the leaf pairs together. Keeping the stalk with the leaves is said to fortify and "feed" the leaves during air-curing. The picked stalk-leaves are draped over long sticks (*cujes*) and dried for twenty-four hours outdoors, then moved into curing barns. These leaves take up much more room in the barns and take up to ninety days to cure (two to three times longer than primed leaves). This technique was more common during the early twentieth century but is rarely used today.

stem (pipe): also referred to as mouthpiece or **bit**, the stem of a pipe incorporates the **lip**, bit, air hole, and **tenon**, which connects to the **briar/meerschaum** at the **shank**.

stemming: either partial or total removal of the stem in a tobacco leaf. Wrappers have the entire stem removed, yielding two separate parts of the leaf; filler leaves have only half the stem removed from the bottom, creating the *pata de rana* ("frog's legs") shape.

Stockholm Cigar Syndrome: the psychological response in cigar sales representatives who fall in love with their own mediocre or bad products. The same can happen to consumers and tobacconists who enjoy a cigar or pipe when they have smoked it with the maker and realize later that it was not nearly as good as they remember. Similarly, **Havana-obsessed consumers** allow themselves to be influenced in their taste perceptions by romance and mythology.

stogie: slang for **cheroot**, named after the cigar making region of Conestoga, PA where the inexpensive cigars were popular with wagon drivers during the 1800s.

straight cut: the flat cut produced by guillotine and double guillotine cigar cutters.

straight grain: a grain pattern found on smooth finish briar pipes with straight line–like markings.

straight pipe: a pipe characterized by a straight **shank** and **stem**. Straight pipes are inclined to transmit more heat directly to the palate than **bent pipes**.

strength (tobacco): the intensity of the nicotine in the cigar or pipe tobacco.

sucker: secondary leaves on tobacco plants that must be removed so nutrients will flow to the primary leaves. Every plant in every field has these "sucker" leaves and they must be meticulously removed by hand.

sugar: the naturally occurring organic compounds found in all tobacco, to varying degrees. Both curing and fermentation can fix and/or develop the sugars in tobacco.

sun-grown: this term refers to tobacco grown in direct sunlight; this intense process creates thicker, more robust leaves, with more pronounced veins.

sun-curing: the process of exposing harvested leaves to direct sunlight; this takes between a few days and a few weeks and releases moisture, preparing the leaf for fermentation. Sun-curing is most commonly used on **Oriental** tobaccos.

sunlight manipulation: while sunlight can be manipulated with **shade** cloth, this term refers to the effect of mountains, surrounding valleys, shading out part of the early and late day sun.

surullo: a small, cigar-like roll of tobacco leaves created from one type of leaf. *Surullos* are used to taste and sample individual leaf types.

tabacalera: Spanish term for cigar factory.

tabaco: Spanish for "tobacco"; synonymous for "cigar" in Cuba.

tabaquero: Spanish term for cigar roller, cigar dealer, or someone in the cigar business.

tabla: the wood surface used by *torcedores* to roll cigars on, made from a very hard wood and placed on top of the rolling table as a work surface.

tallo: Spanish word for stalk or trunk, as it relates to plants.

tamp: the act of gently packing down the tobacco in the bowl of a pipe in order to keep it lit.

tamper: a tool used to pack pipe tobacco. Tampers can be made from any hard, durable material and can range in design from a simple nail-head style to ornate carved and cast versions. Inexpensive tampers can scratch and damage the bowl of a pipe, making softer metals, such as pewter, preferable to discriminating pipe smokers.

tapado: 1) the cheesecloth-like material used to cover shade-grown tobacco; 2) Spanish term for **shade-grown** tobacco.

taste: 1) *noun a:* the human sense that perceives and distinguishes salty, sweet, sour, bitter and **umami** *b*: an individual preference or inclination. 2) *verb*: the act of perceiving and experiencing the flavor (taste+aroma) of something.

taste buds: sensory organs on our tongue which we use to detect the five tastes: salty, sweet, sour, bitter, and umami.

tasting methodology: also referred to as "tasting," this is a simple set of guidelines to follow when evaluating tobacco products: Observation, Description and Comparison, and Evaluation.

Temsco: a type of machine which assists in the cigar filler bunching process, much like a **Lieberman** machine. Cigars which are bunched using the Lieberman or Temsco machine usually have the wrapper applied by hand and are considered premium cigars.

tenon: the projection at the end of the pipe stem that fits into the **mortise** of the bowl.

tercios: palm bark bundles used to package fine tobacco wrappers for aging. The bark is wet down and tightly molded around tobacco piles, tied shut, and then becomes hard like plastic once dried.

terminal threshold: the sensory threshold where saturation inhibits our senses from perceiving any more stimulus; like ten people smoking cigars in a room where the eleventh cigar will not change what you smell.

TobaccAromatherapy: term coined by Tobacconist University in 1998 to describe the beneficial and therapeutic effects of pleasant tobacco aromas.

tobacco beetle: *Lasioderma serricorne*. Found in both food and tobacco, under proper conditions, these eggs can develop into larvae, pupae, and finally adult beetles. During their short lifetime, tobacco beetles can eat through cigars, leaving them ruined and strewn with holes.

tobacconist: an expert dealer in tobacco and the related accoutrements.

tooth: the grainy texture found on some tobacco leaves; mainly Cameroon leaves.

topping: removing the flower from the top of the tobacco plant. This process allows the plant to focus on leaf production.

topping (pipe tobacco): the process of adding a top coat of flavoring to aromatic tobaccos.

torcedor: Spanish term for "cigar roller."

torpedo: a cigar tapered at both the head and the foot.

totalmente a mano: Spanish for "made totally by hand"; hand bunched, bound, no machinery is used.

touch up: the process of evening the burn of a cigar; usually done by lighting the outer wrapper to accelerate the burn rate so the cigar will burn evenly.

trabajar / trabajando: Spanish term meaning "to work / working." Cigar makers refer to fermentation as "working" or "*trabajando*" the *tabaco*.

transplanting: re-planting tobacco seedlings from the *semillero* into the ground.

trichome: very small, hair-like outgrowths found on plant leaves. Tobacco leaves, in addition to being very thick and sticky with resin, have trichomes on their outer surface. The tobacco plant trichomes help the leaf absorb moisture and reflect excessive radiation. After tobacco is rolled into a cigar, the trichomes may still be visible and will help inhibit the evaporation of oils from the cigar's wrapper.

trick pipe: an uncommon or non-traditional pipe that may have some novel or useful feature including folding pipes, pipes with hidden tampers, etc.

tripa: Cuban term for cigar filler tobaccos; literally means "guts."

triple cap: the **parejo** head finishing technique which uses a small tear-drop shaped piece of tobacco woven into the wrapper, to close the open head. After the head is closed, a perfect circle of tobacco (**cap**) is cut with the *casquillo* and placed on top to create a finished look. It is called the triple-cap because the cigar head appears to have several seams.

TSA (Tobacco Settlement Agreements): On November 23, 1998, after years of litigation between state courts and the cigarette industry, leading US cigarette manufacturers signed an agreement with the Attorneys General of forty-six states, five US territories, and the District of Columbia, known as the Master Settlement Agreement, or **MSA**. Previous agreements were already signed with the other four states. Collectively, these agreements are known as the state Tobacco Settlement Agreements, or TSA. These agreements had the effect of making the cigarette industry the most regulated and highly taxed industry in America, and have the unique distinction of making this the only industry legally required to fund its own opposition.

tubo: Spanish for "tube"; *tubos* are used as packaging to help protect cigars.

tunneling: see **canoeing**.

Turkish cigarette: cigarettes made primarily from **Oriental** tobaccos, which are lower in nicotine than **Virginia** tobaccos but convey a rich flavor.

twist: pipe tobacco made from leaves that are twisted together like a rope mimicking the pressing process; see **plug** and **navy cut**.

Umami: the fifth taste, described in Japanese as "deliciousness." Umami is also defined as savory. Specifically, umami is the taste of L-glutamate, the dominant amino acid in living things. Umami taste is common in fermented foods, aged cheese, meat, ketchup, tomatoes, mushrooms, bouillon/broth, soy sauce, MSG, and breast milk.

Uno y Medio: Spanish for "one and a half"; the second level of leaves from the bottom of the **Corojo** plant, just above the **Libre de Pie**.

V cutter: also called a "wedge" or "cat's eye"; this type of cutter digs a wedge-shaped slice out of the head of the cigar.

varietal: a specific and unique seed strain.

varietal family: a broader category which usually includes many specific varietals. In the cigar and pipe tobacco industry, varietal families like **Burley**, **Virginia**, **Oriental**, and **Broadleaf** are often referenced when the actual seed varietals being used are more specific.

vega: the specific plot of land on a farm where tobacco growing takes place.

veguero: 1) Spanish for "plantation worker"; 2) a cigar made from a single tobacco leaf or type of tobacco leaf.

vein: part of a leaf's structure; overly large veins can hinder the viability and attractiveness of wrapper leaves.

vintage: this frequently used term should refer to the year tobacco in a particular cigar or pipe tobacco is harvested. In most cases it will refer to a specific leaf/component like the wrapper or fillers. In the absence of international standards, there is some ambiguity when the term is used; as some cigar makers can misuse the term simply to make their cigars seem older and/or more attractive.

Virginia: also "bright tobacco"; a tobacco varietal that is naturally high in sugar content and typically flue-cured; used in cigarettes and pipe tobaccos.

viso: Spanish term used to describe tobacco leaves from the middle part of the plant. Viso leaves are under Ligero and above Seco leaves.

vitola: the term which describes the specific size and shape characteristics of a cigar within a given brand.

Vitola de Galera: name for a cigar's shape and size as referred to in Cuban cigar factories.

Vitola de Salida: name for a cigar's shape and size in the marketplace.

vitolphilia: the collection and study of cigar bands and labels.

volado: filler leaves from the bottom of the **Criollo** plant. Volado leaves are valued for their mildness and easy burning qualities.

Vulcanite: a hard vulcanized rubber that is widely used in pipe **stems**. Although it is easier on the teeth than other stem materials, vulcanite tends to tarnish more than other materials.

wetting: see **mojo**.

wilde: a cigarillo whose filler leaves protrude from the wrapper at the foot.

wrapper: applied to the outside of the cigar, this is the most delicate, expensive, and (ideally) perfect leaf used in cigar construction. In addition, wrapper leaves contribute significantly to the flavor of the cigar since they are touching the mouth and tongue.

yagua: See **Royal Palm**.

yute: Spanish for "burlap."

zafado: the shaking loose of *gavillas* after they arrive at the factory.

If you would like to learn more, please visit the Tobacconist University (TU) website glossary for a multi-media learning experience; including pictures, video, and enhanced content links. The TU Glossary puts you one click away from our entire academic curriculum and everything you ever wanted to know about luxury tobacco.

RESOURCES

Agronomists

LEONCIO CRUZ MONTERO
Investigador Programa Nacional de Investigaciones en Tabaco
Ingeniero Agrónomo de la Universidad Católica Madre y
  Maestra.
Diplomado en el cultivo del tabaco negro en la Universidad de
  Pinar del Río, Cuba.

Dr. LEONEL FERMIN DIAZ BOMNIN, CA.

Encargado del Programa Nacional de Investigaciones en Tabaco
  del IDIAF
Ingeniero Agrónomo de la Universidad de Pinar del Río, Cuba.
Doctor en Ciencias Agrícolas

Bibliography

Adargelio Garrido De La Grana, *Lo Llamaremos Cohiba: Leyenda De Un Placer* (Habanos S.A., 1997).

Adriano Martinez Rius, *Habano El Rey* (Epicur Publications S.L., 1999).

Antonio Núñez Jiménez, *The Journey of the Havana Cigar* (T.F.H. Publications, Inc., 1988).

Anwer Bati and Simon Chase, *The Cigar Companion: A Connoisseur's Guide* (Quintet Publishing plc, 1995).

B.C. Akehurst, *TOBACCO: Tropical Agricultural Series* (Longmans Green and Co. Ltd., 1968).

Brian and Wilma Rittershausen, *Growing Orchids* (Annes Publishing Limited, 2000).

Bernard Le Roy and Maurice Szafran, *The Illustrated History of Cigars* (Harold Starke Publishers Limited, 1993). (translated from *La Grande Histoire du Cigare* © Flammarion 1989)

Carl Ehwa Jr., *The Book of Pipes & Tobacco* (Random House, Inc., 1974).

Carl O. Sauer, "Indian Food Production in the Caribbean," *Geographical Review* 71:3 (1981): 272–280.

Charles B. Heiser Jr., "Cultivated Plants and Cultural Diffusion in Nuclear America," *American Anthropologist New Series* 67:4 (1965): 930–949.

Donald D. Brand, "The Origin and Early Distribution of New World Cultivated Plants," *Agricultural History* 13:2 (1939): 109–117.

Eric Deschodt and Philippe Morane, *Le Cigare* (Editions Du Regard, 1996).

Eumelio Espino Marrero, *Cuban Cigar Tobacco: Why Cuban Cigars Are The World's Best* (T.F.H. Publications, Inc., 1996).

George Gessert, "Flowers of Human Presence: Effects of Esthetic Values on the Evolution of Ornamental Plants," *Leonardo* 26:1 (1993): 37–44.

Gilbert Lewis, "The Beginning of Civilization in America," *American Anthropologist New Series* 49:1 (1947): 1–24.

Harriet Ziefert and pictures by Amanda Haley, *You Can't Taste a Pickle with Your Ear* (Blue Apple Books, 2002).

Jan G. R. Elferink, "Aphrodisiac Use in Pre-Columbian Aztec and Inca Cultures," *Journal of the History of Sexuality* 9:1/2, January–April 2000, 25–36.

Katharine T. Kell, "Tobacco in Folk Cures in Western Society," *The Journal of American Folklore* 78:038 (1965): 99–114.

Luc Sante, *No Smoking* (Assouline Publishing Inc., 2004).

Macalaster College, /macalester.edu.

Marvin R. Shanken, ed., *Cigar Aficionado's World of Cigars* (Running Press & M. Shanken Communications, Inc., 1996).

MedicineNet.com, medicinenet.com.

Michael Siegel, MD, MPH, Director, Center for Public Accountability in Tobacco Control, Social and Behavioral Sciences Department, Boston University School of Public Health, http://www.tobaccocontrolintegrity.com.

Min Ron Nee, *An Illustrated Encyclopedia of Post-Revolution Havana Cigars* (1995).

National Cigar Museum, cigarhistory.info.

National Institutes of Health, nih.gov.

Paul B. K. Garmirian, PhD, *The Gourmet Guide to Cigars* (Cedar Publications, 1990).

Peter Weston Black, "The Anthropology of Tobacco Use: Tobian Data and Theoretical Issues," *Journal of Anthropological Research* 40:4, Winter 1984, 475–503.

Peter W. Stahl, "Halucinatory Imagery and the Origin of Early South American Figurine Art," *World Archaeology* 18:1 Perspectives in World Archaeology (1986): 134–150.

Professional Friends of Wine, winepros.org.

Professor Tim Jacob, Cardiff University, Smell Research Laboratory, cardiff.ac.uk.

Richard Carleton Hacker, *Rare Smoke: The Ultimate Guide To Pipe Collecting* (Autumngold Publishing, 1999).

Richard Carleton Hacker, *The Ultimate Cigar Book, 4th Edition* (Skyhorse Publishing, 2015)

Richard Kluger, *Ashes to Ashes* (Vintage Books, 1997).

Ronald B. Dixon, "Words for Tobacco in American Indian Languages," *American AnthropologistNew Series* 23:1 (1921): 19–49.

Sander L. Gilman and Zhou Xun, eds. *Smoke: A Global History of Smoking.*

Scientific American, sciam.com.

Stanford J. Newman with James V. Miller, Cigar Family*: A 100 Year Journey In The Cigar Industry* (J.C. Newman Cigar Company, 1999).

Thomas Haberman, "Evidence for Aboriginal Tobaccos in Eastern North America," *American Antiquity* 49:2 (1984): 269–287.

Thomas M. Whitmore and B.L. Turner II, "Landscapes of Cultivation in Mesoamerica on the Eve of the Conquest," *Annals of the Association of American Geographers* 82:3 The Americas Before and After 1492: Current Geographical Research (1992): 402–425.

US Food and Drug Administration, fda.gov.

Wine Spectator Online, winespectator.com.

Wine Spectator School, winespectatorschool.com.

Zino Davidoff, *The Connoisseur's Book of the Cigar* (McGraw-Hill, 1984).

Editing
R. Sloane Franklin, CRT

Illustrations
Kathryn Bellando, CRT

Research and Studies
Differential Neural Responses Evoked by Orthonasal versus Retronasal Odorant Perception in Humans

Dana M. Small (Yale University and The John B. Pierce Laboratory), Johannes C. Gerber (University of Dresden Medical School), Erica Mak (The John B. Pierce Laboratory), and Thomas Hummel (University of Dresden Medical School)

Neuron, Vol. 47, 593–605 August 18, 2005, Copyright 2005 by Elsevier Inc.

The Influence of Saliva on pH Changes in the Mouth

Y. Suzuki, and S. Watanabe, Meikai University, Sakado, Japan

Organizations and People
A Little Taste of Cuba
Brian Berman
Camacho Cigars
Cigar Rights of America
Cubatabaco
David J. Berkebile and Georgetown Tobacco
GMAC Creative: Gayle Macdonell
Golden Film Production and Photography
Guillermo Leon
PCA/IPCPR/RTDA
J. Glynn Loope

Jonathan Drew
Jose "Pepin" Garcia
Juan Diaz-Tenorio
La Aurora: Jose Blanco
Lia Costabile
Michael Dixon Humidors
Michael Herklots, CMT
National Cigar Museum
Paul B.K. Garmirian, PhD
Piloto Cigars / Padrón Cigars: the entire Padrón family
Rene Castaneda, CST
Steve Saka
United States Department of Agriculture
Xikar

Photo Credits

A Little Taste of Cuba
JLA, CMT
Laura A. Roberts

Video Credits

Tobacconist University
JLA, CMT
R. Sloane Franklin, CRT
Kathryn Bellando, CRT

ACKNOWLEDGMENTS

I would like to thank many individuals without whom Tobacconist University would not exist, starting with my family for their love and support; my beloved mentor and friend J.O.P., the greatest cigar maker I ever knew; every tobacconist, good and bad, that I have ever met; immense gratitude goes to every one of the over one thousand Certified Tobacconists (past and present) who have contributed to the content of this course and their own, as well as the public's education; the thousands of individuals and companies who have purchased, read, and shared *The Tobacconist Handbook* since its first publication in 2009; and, finally, to the thousands of customers and luxury tobacco lovers who teach and challenge us every day. Ultimately, the luxury tobacco industry can only be as great as the tobacconists who serve and fight for it.